Darling Andrew

I we.
happy, it — is great
hope of fun + following
your heart + makes
you laugh!

WITHOUT PREJUDICE

VALERIE MAIR

Thank you —
you. I love
Gran
xxx

Copyright © 2007 Valerie Mair

First printing: 2007, Blitzprint, Calgary, Alberta.
Second printing: 2009, Bennett & Hastings Publishing, Seattle WA
All rights reserved. No part of the contents of this book may
be reproduced without the written permission of the author.

ISBN: 978-1-934733-41-7

CONTENTS

Early Childhood.................................7
Granny Gage...................................14
Granny Plumb..................................22
Grandpa Plumb................................26
Mummy..31
Charles Plumb.................................34

Wartime.......................................49
Teenage Years..................................58
1949 -1953....................................61
Paris 1953.....................................65
1954 -1959....................................69
Marriage.......................................80

Photos...88

Coming to Canada 1966.......................110
Vancouver, British Columbia..................114
Kingston, Ontario..............................118
Toronto, Ontario...............................124
Back to British Columbia......................141
Lucy - Poetry..................................149
Sophie...153
Sri Sathya Sai Baba............................159

Ancestral History:
The Cutting Family.............................164
The Gage Family................................169
The Holmes Family.............................173
The Moule Family..............................179
The Plumb Family..............................182

Bibliography...................................184

ABOUT THIS BOOK

This book is about families and souls and my journey. I wanted to pay tribute to those who have gone before us and left their legacies of inspiration and courage. I thank everyone in my life who has kept me company along the way.

Maeve Binchy, my favourite author, has been to Vancouver more than once and encouraged everyone to write. "Write from the heart, write what you know, write as you speak" she told us. Thank you, Maeve Binchy.

Finally, a quote from Shakespeare's Benedick in *Much Ado About Nothing* (Scene III):

"For man is a giddy thing, and this is my conclusion."

EARLY CHILDHOOD

Mary Gage and Charles Plumb married in Belfast in February 1931. I was born on May 14, 1932. We lived in Eglantine Gardens, Belfast, then moved to Lisaven, a big house in Holywood. Granny Gage lived at Felden in Whitehouse. When I was a few weeks old she announced an emergency christening as my parents were going on a bicycling trip. I would go with Molly McGreevy, their maid, to her mother's cottage in the Mountains of Mourne, and could become 'a wee papist.'

I heard endless discussions about Catholics and Protestants, but the 'English' fascinated me the most; these 'English' must surely be aliens, maybe even robots. So when I was four and went to London, I was amazed to see normal people.

Life was very lonely. I hardly saw my parents, so I found things to do. I learned to read with the book *The Cat Sat on The Mat.* There were only twenty six letters in the alphabet, and that book explained each one, so it was just a matter of putting words together. I lived in books. Mostly fairy tale books and later the Arthur Ransome books and many others. Arthur Ransome was my favourite author. I cried my eyes out over David Copperfield. Maybe it was a children's version.

It was thrilling when they told me I was going to have a sister. I imagined a little girl exactly like me. On the day Juliet was born, February 20, 1935, my grandfather took me to see her in his little Morris car. I had on my best dress and black patent leather shoes and felt so happy. It was a shock to see this tiny squealing baby who was supposed to be my playmate and friend. I felt betrayed and furious. My mother put me in the corner for sulking.

My father worked for the North of Ireland government and read the news every day. He always came to say good night, and see what I was reading. I loved the smell of his tweed suit and pipe. My parents had lots of parties and the most awful fights. It was terrifying. I had my own room, and Juliet slept in the nursery. One day Granny took us to the zoo. The lions had given

EARLY CHILDHOOD

birth, and the keeper let me hold one of the cubs. Later I heard the lions had killed their cubs, and I worried that our parents might kill us. I had a little pottie and my worst fear was that I would be out of bed, and they might rush in, take my arms and split me in half. I planned to roll into a ball, and pretend to be asleep; then they might not bother.

The anxiety was always there, and impossible to talk about. Juliet was barely a toddler. My two grandmothers were wonderful. I knew they loved me, but they were not there at the time, and I did not dare to tell them. I didn't see how they could save me.

Nursemaids did not stay long. Just as soon as you trusted one of them, she would go on her night off and never come back. We had a lovely house with a huge garden and played outside all the time, but did not know any other children. We had fun hanging around the kitchen, listening to the chat. The gardener poured his tea into his saucer. I was in awe. I would have given all my toys to be allowed to do that, but knew I would get into terrible trouble.

When we went to visit Granny Gage we had a lot more fun as often our cousins Gillian and Bill Gage were staying nearby. I wasn't afraid at Felden. I talked to Granny and pestered her about everything. She was so patient and never got tired of explaining. She taught me to do sums and to sew, and kept us busy every minute learning something or other. She took me into Belfast in her Morris car. It was bigger than Grandpa's. Her gardener lived at one gate, and the chauffeur at the other. Everybody around Granny was kept busy. She was involved in the Mothers' Union and the Church. I never saw her just sitting down. She worked all the time, often on her hands and knees in the garden wearing her overalls and her hat.

I went to a big school near Lisaven when I was four. We wore a navy uniform, and I was the smallest child there. I was petrified and far too shy to talk to anyone at all, but I did like the school work. One day the headmistress took me on her lap, and explained that if I did not speak I could not stay at the school. That afternoon we were going to learn some needlework I was

EARLY CHILDHOOD

dying to do, so I promised her with all my heart that I would talk after lunch. This was huge for me, and I knew I had the courage to do it, no matter what happened. When I got home to lunch Granny's car was at the door loaded with luggage. My heart just dropped. I was devastated. We were leaving, to stay with her, and I would not be going back to the school. I felt I had let my headmistress down and had not been true to myself. I could not tell anyone about it, not even my grandmother. I felt so guilty and ashamed.

We must have stayed at Felden for quite awhile as Granny found a governess to give us lessons. The governess was cruel. One day she held my hand and ran so fast that I flew through the rose bushes. When Granny saw me covered in scratches, I told her what had happened, but she became furious with me for telling such a lie. The governess insisted that I had stupidly run into the bushes as I didn't look where I was going. Maybe she showed her true colours, as she left quite soon after that. I went to share lessons with Cynthia and Mark McFerren, which was fun: it was a sort of mini-school for the three of us.

My grandfather, William Charles Gage, was a darling gentle man, full of love and serenity and peace. He was a solicitor in Belfast and got along with everybody. He seemed to be the only quiet person in the family. Granny nagged him.

She would cry, "Willie Willie, do this do that," and he just did whatever she said. He walked for hours on end whistling the hymn "The Church's One Foundation." I loved going with him. We walked in total silence one behind the other. I was full of thoughts, he whistled, and we were happy. Once I tripped and knocked a tooth out, as I had my hands in my pockets like him. Granny was cross with him, and I felt so sorry to have gotten him into trouble. Grandpa Gage was always there: loving us, buying us toys, coming to say good night. When we had measles he watched over us every night. I was content at Felden with Granny and Grandpa. It was safe there. She put us to bed and waited outside the door until we were nearly asleep. Then she went downstairs to play the piano, lovely Chopin and Beethoven sonatas and preludes.

EARLY CHILDHOOD

Once we were in the cake shop in Belfast. The window was full of delicious cakes perched on tall stands. I leaned on the glass I thought was there and brought all the cakes down like ninepins. I was horrified, but Granny just paid for them as if nothing had happened.

At Christmas she took me to the sick children in hospital to help her give them presents. I wanted to talk to them and ask why they were there, but never got a chance. When visitors came to tea we were only allowed to come into the drawing room to meet them for a few minutes after tea. We had to be seen and not heard!

In 1937, after their coronation, the King and Queen came over to Belfast with Princess Elizabeth and Princess Margaret. We went to see the parade in Belfast and in the evening watched the royal yacht sail away. My father had to be really well dressed and wear his top hat. My mother had jumped on it and broken it in a rage. This sort of thing was always happening. Once he went out and left Mummy locked in her room. She kept calling me to let her out and was furious when I wouldn't. I don't know whether I didn't know where the key was, or if I was scared of her coming out and blaming me because she had been locked in. I felt everything was my fault, and was sure that they would be supremely happy and content had they not had me.

When Mummy had her friends over they would laugh and talk. Someone would see me lurking about and say, "Is that Valerie? She is very plain isn't she." I thought that was a silly thing to say. Why did she not say I was ugly or pretty. 'Plain' meant nothing. I felt like a biscuit! Deep down I thought I was an ugly duckling. I didn't fit in anywhere. I still did not have a friend my own age, as Gillian was Juliet's age and Bill was even younger. And I knew that I didn't belong in my cousins' world. My mother would say, "You are not a Gage. You are a Plumb."

All my life I had been searching for God. I wanted to feel close to God. Granny took me to the Anglican Church and I listened to the sermons. Somehow I felt there must be more than what I was hearing. One night either I had a dream, or I got out of bed and

EARLY CHILDHOOD

came down to the study where we always had afternoon tea. I am sure I actually did this because the study felt warm and cosy, it was dark, the clock was ticking and the coals were still crackling in the fireplace. I looked out, and there was Jesus walking in the garden. There was a great light around him, and I felt so happy and full of joy that he was real, and that he would always be with me no matter what happened. I never told anybody.

We went to London for a short time. It was exciting catching the boat from Belfast to Heysham and then a night train to London. I was very scared when we went in the Underground. The trains rumbled in the distance, then roared into the station. I didn't like that time in London. There was a lot of fog so it was spooky. Someone took me to the swings and roundabouts in a park. Whoever it was forced me to go on the roundabouts when I said I did not want to, and I was very sick. One day when I was five I looked at my fingers and knew that I was not just five. I knew I was millions of years old, though I couldn't remember any other lives. On my fifth birthday a taxi arrived and a huge Black Labrador puppy leaped out and knocked me flat on my back. We loved her and called her Chloe.

I don't remember actually leaving Ireland but when I was six we were in a house at Boxhill in Surrey. One night whoever was in charge called Granny to say she had no money. Uncle Conolly and Aunt Nancy came and drove us, through the night, to their house. When I woke up people were arriving and arguing about issuing writs. Our parents were eventually divorced by a special Act of Parliament in the North of Ireland called Plumb's Divorce Act, 1939. "An Act to dissolve the marriage of Mary Violet Plumb of Felden, Whitehouse, in the County of Antrim with Charles Theodore Plumb her husband and to enable her to marry again, and for other purposes. (29th March, 1939)." After that we were made Wards of Chancery Court.

Another miserable time was when Mummy took us to England and left us in a foster home in Portsmouth, while she went and looked for a house. I thought we would be there for only a day or two. I lay in bed listening to my mother talking to the lady, waiting for her to come and kiss us good night, but she

11

EARLY CHILDHOOD

never came. I was desolate thinking she would never come back. It was a dreadful time. The women were cruel to all the children. Nobody could have water except for one glass at each meal. They smacked a little boy in a high chair because he couldn't eat his boiled egg properly. I had never felt so abandoned. It seemed to go on for weeks. Poor Juliet got into more trouble than I did and I tried to protect her. It was a terrible worry. The other children were from Liverpool, and when my mother came back we had Liverpool accents.

My poor mother was caught in the middle of all her troubles. She fought with her husband and she fought with her mother, so she probably did not want to leave us with Granny while she went off to England. Also the divorce proceedings were going through. She must have thought she had found a safe place for us in the meantime. A friend tells me it sounded like somewhere his mother left him when she went to India, and it was highly recommended.

Mummy took us to Penselwood in Somerset, miles from any-where, with wonderful woods and fields in which we could play. There were lots of adders about, big grey snakes and we were terrified of them. At lunch one day Juliet said, "There is a snake." We didn't believe her, as she was so little, and an enormous snake was wriggling under the door to the larder. If she hadn't seen it we would have gone in there and been bitten. When our gardener came back from lunch he shot it. Another day I trod on a snake in the field. It shot up my leg and I ran, leaving little Juliet standing there in her lacy bonnet. I still feel guilty at not having had the presence of mind to take her with me. Juliet and I fought a lot, but I felt my mission in life was to take care of her, so I worried a lot. If Mummy was still asleep when we got up in the morning, I got on a chair, lit the gas stove and cooked scrambled eggs for us.

We were at Penselwood when I first met my second cousin Jocelyn Hogg, who was eight at the time. Her mother, Olivia, was the only child of Uncle Willie, Granny's elder brother, who had lost his leg in the Boer War. Olivia and my mother were first cousins and good friends, and wanted us to be good friends too.

EARLY CHILDHOOD

She came up to my room where I was deep in a book called *Jewel*. I said I would come and play with her, but I had to finish my chapter first. Maybe it is no wonder I was lonely.

Jocelyn and I became life-long friends and spent many happy weekends together in Yattendon, Berkshire, playing endless games of Monopoly™, riding bikes, jumping off trees and so on. Her brothers, Jeremy and Adam, were there too. They were a happy self-confident family. Jeremy and Jocelyn looked alike, and Adam was an appealing little boy with freckles. I felt comfortable with him. Jocelyn was everything I was not. She was very articulate, outgoing, and good at everything she did. I really admired her and so did my mother who wailed, "Why can't you be more like Jocelyn?" I liked Jocelyn coming to stay, as she was a buffer between me and my mother and could talk intelligently about everything. I knew I could never measure up to her, but I loved being her friend. When I went to stay I felt intimidated by Olivia, but enjoyed listening to all the conversations. Jocelyn died of cancer in 2003. Adam and Anne, his wife, lived in Paris, and we kept in touch. Sadly, Anne died in her sleep in 2007. Then in August 2008, soon after he had called me, Adam died suddenly of a heart attack. I have lost touch with Jeremy.

I don't know where Mummy met Dick Nicholson, whom she married, but we met him when he came to Penselwood. He took us to a circus. We thought it was wonderful, and that he was wonderful too. He made Mummy happy and that was the most important thing.

GRANNY GAGE

Granny Gage was the most important person in my life. She was always there for us. Although she was tough and strict, and didn't really cuddle and kiss us, we felt secure with her. I had her to thank for everything I knew: she taught me how to read and write, how to do arithmetic, and how to handle money. I loved the smells in her herb and vegetable garden and the delicious aroma of food cooking in her kitchen.

She was terrified we would be taken out of the country, and so she made us Wards of Chancery Court. This meant that until we reached twenty one years of age we could not leave the British Isles without the Court's permission.

I found a remarkable letter that Granny wrote to my poor mother when Mother was separated from her husband and utterly miserable. It is certainly not heartwarming. I cannot imagine how those grandparents produced someone like me; with my sentimental, romantic, bursting-into-tears personality. My great grandmother, Olivia Holmes (Granny Gage's mother) was more like me, I think. This letter would have depressed me dreadfully.

Here is the letter from May Gage to her daughter Mary Plumb, dated September 21 (probably 1937) from Felden:

> Dearest Mary,
>
> Some of your posts come quite quickly, as I got the letter you posted yesterday today. I am glad you seem to be seeing or going to see more company this week, but I daresay the majority of people don't see much company and they get on all right. If a person is occupied and interested in something they don't need to be always 'cracking', and English people are much more inclined to occupy themselves and less inclined to crack with neighbours than Irish people are. I always imagine it is my English blood that makes

me not mind being left alone. Mrs. Bell is always wanting to know am I not lonely but even she has now come to say "Oh you don't mind being alone." I never want to be running down to the Hut or Glassalreedanl or to the Bates as the rest of the family do, and here I am quite alone now with Daddy in Rosapenna and I don't dislike it. Mrs. Cornish is a great deal alone - the day she was here she stayed till 7.30 and her husband was not coming home till 9. He goes out at 9 in the morning and those are his hours 3 days a week and she is English and a stranger in Belfast. She said "I rather like being alone." I don't really feel lonely. Personally I would feel much more lonely with a restless or an uncongenial person than I ever would be alone. I think your nerves are all in such an abnormal condition that you will never be content until you have got them under control and have come to have some real belief in the reason for your existence and the importance of the duties that you have to do. It makes all the little daily jobs seem no longer trivial and bothersome if you know they have to be done and that you can do them and nobody else has exactly the same task. As long as you are looking after your children you are doing one of the most important works in the world. And those children will remember what they have seen you do and heard you say long after you are dead. And so what you do and say never really dies. Lots of things my father said to me have far more meaning to me now than they had when he said them. Lily may mind the children all right for the present but they are only an episode in HER life. She may have to leave them any minute but the responsibility for them is yours and you can't get rid of it. And I don't think you should want to.

GRANNY GAGE

About going back to Charles I have never claimed any right to dictate. The complaints you have made about him were quite voluntary. I have never asked to be told, but one thing is VERY clear and that is that if you do go back to him for the rather contemptible reason that you find life by yourself monotonous, I shall have been made a greater fool of than any woman I have known. And to anyone who knows the circumstances I should think it would be amply obvious that you and Charles had very cleverly exploited both Daddy and me for your own ends. It is not even as if it was the first time it has happened. This is the THIRD year that you and he have quarrelled over an orgy of self-indulgence and advertised it to the whole town, causing pain, trouble and expense to friends and relations all round. To give Charles his due it is quite easy to understand it from his point of view. He openly professed a creed of Hedonism, which means the pursuit of pleasure --and as he has to acknowledge that over-indulgence in any form of pleasure leads to satiety after a time, it follows that he must employ some means to whip up appetite again to enjoy that pleasure once more. When a man with his belief has enjoyed living with his wife till he begins to tire—what better way of whipping up physical appetite than by going after some other and quarrelling with his wife, having rows, separations, scandals, excitements, and final reconciliation, leading to renewed enjoyment. If one does not happen to be a Hedonist, however, this simply seems very revolting. And to a wife I should think it would always be very unsatisfactory, as it would always come to HER being left for good in the end, and she would have suffered much more than the man in the process.

Charles has never concealed his ideas and

16

opinions, and you now know very well how these work out in practice. So if you go back to him you know what you are doing. I used to think on other occasions that you might really want to make him better and that you would try. But now I know that that is not so but that the whole thing will be over and over again, so that I am determined that as far as I am concerned Charles Plumb shall not make a fool of ME again. It is not a bad idea from his point of view to get himself relieved of a troublesome infant for nearly a year. To have both his children kept and cared for and clothed almost altogether by his old mother-in-law, and then to get rid of wife and children without the slightest trouble or expense to himself for six months, leaving him free as air to enjoy himself until he feels inclined to beckon his wife back again, and doubtless enjoy a good laugh at the expense of the people he has fooled. Professor Lowry, Dr. Rankin, the respectable and hoary solicitors and best of all, old fools of pa-in-law and tight-lipped ma-in-law and hosts of friends and relations.

As far as Charles is concerned he comes out top all round and is much to be congratulated on his superior intelligence. There will be no blame to him. All Belfast will be given to understand that his wife drank so much that he could not keep her and she could not mind her children, and that her parents were forced by circumstances to take her away and look after her and provide for her for six months—and that he is wonderfully forbearing to take her back. Of course as far as the general public are concerned they could hardly believe anything else, because IF your complaints are true and our version of the matter were correct, no decent woman would or could go back and no parents would be such idiots as to provide all

GRANNY GAGE

the money time after time to restore a daughter in order for her to go back and begin again. That should be Charles' affair entirely if he cannot keep you in order himself. You will certainly not find him improved by his six-months' free life. So if you do go back I think you were very foolish to have left him. You will probably find both him and your house very deteriorated and probably the servants won't care for a mistress again after being on their own so long. They will give notice and you will be back this Christmas where you were last only with this difference that there will no longer be Felden to fall back on. In any case Daddy and I were intending to go away this Christmas, and we have been thinking seriously of giving up this place. I am getting very old and tired and this house and place is too big for me to look after especially since my eyes have failed so badly. I can hardly read now and I find gardening difficult.

I have lost heart in things too and I can see that all these worries about you and the children have taken a lot of the fun out of Daddy. He seems to dislike going to the club now and is not very keen about cracking with anybody. I know he has felt all along that you were not being straight about things, and I know he thinks I am foolish to have done all I have for you. However, I don't regret that—if you said you wanted a fresh start I was bound to help you to one, even if it was to be no good. Only if you come back I think I would rather be away out of this. Conolly and Nancy can never be much here as years go on and even if you are in Belfast we should not see much of you. Charles shall NEVER come here again, and it is better for all of us that the children should not come either.

Sometimes I think Daddy might retire and we might end our days ourselves in some little country place round London. I think Daddy will be quite happy now doing nothing and perhaps playing a little golf now and then with Conolly. He MUST retire sometime, he cannot go on working forever, he would be too old to be any good, and I cannot work as I have done for much longer THAT is quite certain. I suppose you will call this a sermon, but it is not that because I preach nothing to you. I only point out how MY position stands. When Daddy and I were married our whole lives and work were centred in and inspired by our children. We looked forward to everything through and for them and what they were going to be. It is impossible to read-just one's outlook at our time of life. We always saw the future through the children's lives that we felt were going to carry on ours and when they fail us there is no future to see.

Love from Mother

I must say I am glad I was not her daughter. I would never have fulfilled her expectations. I'd have torn the letter into shreds and screamed at her, pointing out that *she* was NOT alone, that *she had* Daddy, emotional security and a stable life.

But I felt closer to Granny all the time and could barely wait for the school holidays, when I would see her again. When I started working, I was able to spend weekends with her in the country, and she laughed when I told her about my adventures. Most of them, anyway...

She was less amused on a day the butcher's boy delivered her order when she was out, and I convinced this innocent red-haired boy that I could drive. He let me drive the van, and of course we ended up in a ditch. The butcher was inconvenienced, having to call all his customers, and Granny was furious with me, especially as she said I was "bursting in a most unseemly way" out of

GRANNY GAGE

my cotton dress. There was no damage to the van, and I begged her to tell the butcher it was all my fault. Fortunately, she was never angry with me for long.

She wrote the following letter to her nephew, James Henry, after my mother was widowed in 1944:

Bawnmore, Yately, Nr. Camberley, Hants
July 31st, 1944

Dear Jim,

Thank you from my heart for your letter. I know your thought of her will help Mary in her bitter sorrow. She writes very bravely, but I know she is heart broken. They were so devoted to each other, and he was one of the best and gentlest men I ever met. I had grown to love him myself—he never seemed to have a thought of himself in anything.

DO come over if you can any time, it will be the greatest pleasure to see you, and if you can stay a night and bring Susan. June Murphy came over last Friday and I felt better after she had left. A little chat does take one's mind from brooding over sorrow which is unhealthy for body and soul.

Never let your faith falter, Jim; there was never a time in the world when it was so much needed. I don't know how difficult it may seem to the young people in these awful days, but I DO know that if one clings to faith it becomes clearer and brighter as the years go by. In old age it is the only thing that matters; and things that were so hard to understand and to bear in youth become so much easier. It is as if the veil between this world and the next begins to lift and events fall into a new proportion. I have come to feel that difference in creeds and nationalities are only

20

of this world. The army of the faithful are to be found in them all; and they alone can stand untouched by any of the world's tumults.

Thank you again for writing; I have thought a great deal of your troubles and suffering too, and may God bless you and your wife and grant you a bright future.

Your affectionate

Aunt May

Granny was born on June 27th, 1873 and died, shortly after my twenty-first birthday, in May 1953.

GRANNY PLUMB

Emma May Plumb. We called her Gran Gran. She said one was for her and one for Grandpa who had died in 1930. She was a beautiful, tall lady; very kind, patient and loving. I never saw her get annoyed or excited or emotional. She was a nurse before she married Charles Edward Plumb. They had Charles in 1905 and Margaret in 1909. She simply adored everyone. Especially her Theodore, as she called Charles.

During the war she had a flat in Maida Vale in London. One night when Charles was there, he heard his mother mutter, "MICE, again!" Bombs were dropping all around.

We visited her in nursing homes. She seemed to be bedridden for years, loving us and everybody until the end, though she suffered agonizing back pain. Her doctor said, "Her heart is sound; it beats like a guardsman's drum." Her solicitor worried because she wrote cheques to everybody when she did not have the money. He wrote to Charles:

> I am glad to hear your Mother has got over the recent upset but it is a pity that she still has the hallucination that she is a wealthy woman. So long as she confines her writing of 5,000 (pound sterling) cheques in your favour or Margaret's no desperate harm will be done but it might be more awkward if she sends them to out-siders!
>
> P.S. CONFIDENTIAL. I saw in yesterday's *Daily Mail* that a Dr. Creditor had been involved in a case with an old lady and it was alleged that he had exercised undue influence and had made out her Will in which his name had been substituted for that of a relative for a legacy of 12,000 (pounds sterling). I do not know what the result of the case will be but whatever the rights or wrongs may be I merely mention it as I think we

ought to be particularly careful as I assume he is
the same doctor as is attending your mother!

My grandfather was away a great deal of the time, so the
family kept in touch by writing letters. Here is a letter Gran
Gran wrote to her husband from St. Cyr in France on March
28th, 1928:

> My Beloved,
>
> Charles has gone into Tours and I am to meet
> him there at four o'clock and shall possibly see
> Margaret also when she comes from the Institute
> at 4.15. The cold spell here still continues and it
> is very disappointing for, somehow—when cold
> and grey, it is very cold and grey. The blossom-
> ing trees lose so much of their beauty against a
> grey background, whilst a blue one would make
> just all the difference. There is a huge cherry
> tree smothered in white blossom now, but asking
> for blue sky to show up its full beauty. The house
> too is so cold. However, we hope it will soon
> pass. My fur coat is such a comfort, and so is
> every other warm thing. Our weather changed
> with the coming of the new moon a week ago
> today. Our boy is NOT WELL; i.e. not actually
> downright ill, but never really properly well. He
> is white and looks drawn and tired. He does not
> like 'this show' at all at all. He petrifies with cold
> etc. He has had some internal pain—not bad—
> but there mostly, complains of his legs feeling
> wobbly, and of getting suddenly so tired, etc. i.e.
> of general malaise. I feel sure he ought to see
> a good doctor and be thoroughly over-hauled—
> but cannot arrange it here.
>
> He is much puzzled about the future—what to
> do? How to do it! Whether to enter his name for
> T.C.S. Examination in May (it has to be done in
> May if he takes the exam in August), or whether

GRANNY PLUMB

to wait and see how he does in his Schools (but then he cannot take the T.C.S. Exam in August). Above all else he wants to see you, to talk everything well out. "I must see Father" he says "and talk"—for it simply is impossible to write. "But, how is it to be done?." I suggested that when he was as far north as Seathwaite Broughton-in-Furness perhaps you two could arrange to meet somewhere? He jumped at this, and said did I think you could come over and see him there for a weekend, or middle week, or anything? Most of June is taken up with 'Schools.' He has to return to Oxford for his Viva in July. The T.C.S. Exams would take up most of August, he would have to be in London. After Schools he would have work to prepare for his Viva, and after that to work for T.C.S. It is a bit stiff and a case of "Life is one -------thing after another!

He seems worried and anxious and not at all happy one way and another. Partly health (I am certain) and partly not being able to see his way and feeling he never can without consulting with you.

"I MUST see Father!"

You will have to see if you cannot arrange something, and it must be before you go away in April, as after you come back it will be too late. The great excitement in Tours is that the Tour de Charlemagne fell yesterday; i.e. one half of it from top to bottom as though cleft with a hatchet. The half that remains is gaping with cracks and an expert from Paris decided it must be dynamited slowly, and bit by bit. This is to be done this evening. The Tower stands in crowded streets with shops and houses all round about to say nothing of St. Martins. No-one was about fortunately when it fell, or rather crumbled, and not a soul was hurt nor a window broken, and if you could see just where it stands and how narrow the old streets and how crammed and crowded up, you would agree that the age of miracles still continues. It is very sad to lose this old Tower, built by Charlemagne over the tomb of his third wife. Only last Sunday some girls climbed the Tower!!! To look at Tours from that perspective. Little they knew the danger they ran. On 'Lady Day' I went to a service at St. Julian. It is also an old church and very beautiful. The service was special for the day and all in Latin. I loved it, even although I could not understand much of it. I thought how YOU would have rejoiced in it, and also the added joy of being able to follow the Latin easily.

Many happy returns of the day, i.e. of March 25th and the anniversary also of your Consecration.

Much love dearest,
Your own wife May

GRANDPA PLUMB

My paternal grandfather was born in 1865 and died in 1930. In my mind, he was a shadowy figure who lived a good and blameless life. Saddened that I never met this man, I asked Gran Gran about him. The following information is taken from *The Scottish Chronicle* of December 5, 1930. I have rewritten it.

> Charles Edward Plumb appeared to be an able and clear-headed man, wise and sane in judgment, deeply spiritual and full of humour and friendliness. Though he loved books it is said he loved people more. He studied at Litchfield Theological College and at Oxford where he gained one of the two first class degrees awarded in his year. He eventually became Principal of St. Stephen's College, Oxford.

> The next period of his life brought him to Scotland. He was in charge of St. Margaret's, Braemar, from 1897 to 1906. In 1906 he was appointed Provost of St. Ninian's Cathedral, Perth; then in 1908 he was elected Bishop of St. Andrews, Dunkeld, and Dunblane. One of the people he confirmed was Lady Elizabeth Bowes-Lyon in 1917.

All this took its toll on his psyche. The spiritual path is not an easy one. It can become a lonely desert. Grandpa Plumb had plenty of difficulties during his Episcopate, which gave him many sleepless nights, and he was by nature a worrier. At one point his health broke down and he actually resigned the See. He made a miraculous recovery and was able to carry on for four years, but had a nervous breakdown early in 1930.

Throughout his life in the Church he was a trusted leader, accessible to anyone who needed to speak to him, and always ready to help. I think he must have had to put his own family on

26

GRANDPA PLUMB

the back burner in order to deal with the endless demands. From the many letters his son wrote, I am sure that his son (who would become my father) felt a great gulf in their relationship. It seems my father needed his father, but could not reach him.

Below are three letters Grandpa Plumb wrote to his wife. (Note that they always called my father, Charles, by his second name, Theodore.)

Ashchurch, Saturday, July 14, 1917

My Dearest,

I have a nice little gossip from you this morning as well as a wire about Grant which is quite satisfactory and various other letters. You had a strenuous day at St. Andrews and I shall hope to hear more about it when I come home, but am disappointed that Singer is out of court.

I am very glad indeed to hear that Mrs. Everard is so much better and also that Miss H has got her house at last. I should like to give Madeline E something nice and will see if I have the chance of bringing anything. But that depends upon whether I can get any time in York on my return journey and I don't know yet how that will work out. My present intention is to come home on Friday but everything is somewhat uncertain.

I am much enjoying a quiet and restful time here—the weather is beautiful, and we sit in the garden, or bicycle to see the neighbouring villages and churches, or to Tewkesbury to shop— and one forgets most of the time the anxieties of the diocese. You had better send letters of Monday Tuesday and Wednesday (forenoon) to Miss Plumb, Adlington House, Terrington St. Clement, Kings Lynn. I don't want the whole district to know I am there so I want you to select

27

them and put them in an envelope and address them as above without my name at all. You will need to weigh them carefully to ascertain postage for you sent me some today which were much overstamped. (underlined)

Lots of love from us all
  Your loving husband, Charlie

❀ ❀ ❀

Ashchurch, Monday July 16, 1917

My darling Wife,

  This is a day of heavy thunder showers after a lovely week of sunshine and our plans are rather upset. Yesterday was beautiful and you will be amused to hear how I spent it. I celebrated and attended a sung celebration at Tewkesbury Abbey—preached here at 11'oc and again at the Abbey at Evensong. The vicar sent a motor for me and Helen went in too and stayed for supper and much enjoyed it all: and so did I though I did not mean to preach twice. In the afternoon I wrote a lot of letters and have spent most of this morning at it too. I received the last pattern from you today of green and gold and think it very handsome. I have ordered a frontal of it with the rose and crown green plush for a dorsal and it will look very well: so that is settled. I shall try to visit Inverkeithny on Friday on my way home, and finish up other odds and ends, but we shall not get everything in order for the 29th. I had a note from Canon Meredith today in consequence of which I propose to go to Crieff and confirm on July 25. Next Sunday Callarder, 29th Rosyth, August 4 Glenalmond and the following three Sundays at Pitlochry.

GRANDPA PLUMB

I hope all goes well with you and that you
have recovered from your strenuous day at St.
Andrews. I leave here at 9.15 tomorrow and
arrive at Terrington about 4'oc leaving again on
Thursday and getting home on Friday, at least I
hope so: and shall be very glad to get back again
though I have enjoyed the time here. The posts
are so inconvenient that it almost comes to two
days each way and it is very difficult to make my
plans and arrangements for Rosyth. You would
love the roses and fruit and vegetables here in
such abundance, and the scents and sounds of
the country are delicious.

Love to you all

Your loving husband, Charlie

❋❋❋

From The Rectory, Crieff, Scotland
14th October 1917

My darling wife,

I got back on Friday night and found your
preparations most complete and convenient and
made myself most comfortable both for supper
and breakfast. The only thing I did not understand was the lettuce!

I came away at 12.15 and we had a very pleasant afternoon and today Theodore came to lunch
and goes back when I go to Evening service. I
suppose I shall go home tomorrow eve and after
that I am uncertain because I forgot to ask you
what arrangements you had made with Mrs.
Don—so perhaps I may come to you on Tuesday
11.30 and stay the night: so as to make my plans
for the week and also hear the first of the Giffon
lectures. *Mais nous verrons.*

29

GRANDPA PLUMB

I have ordered all my letters this week to go to the Cathedral. Tomorrow I may go to C. to see Mr. Speir and go home in the evening, getting some dinner at the station. They have made me very comfortable at the Rectory—with a fire in the bedroom we occupied together—and we are living in the little room next to the study. It has been a beautiful sunny day but spoiled for me by a headache in spite of a cachet after breakfast. Now I must give a little attention to Theodore.

Please give some of the kisses to Margaret.

Your loving husband,
　Charlie

MUMMY

Mary Violet Gage was born in Dublin to William and May Gage on January 21, 1907. She loved life when she was young and was always up to mischief. She went to the same school Granny went to, the Queen Alexandra School in Dublin.

She wrote this hilarious letter to my father in 1940 after she married Dick Nicholson:

> I got instant dismissal from the factory because I put in the suggestion box that if women did the same amount of work as men they should be allowed to smoke as much. I worked in the Experimental Drawing Office with a lot of qualified engineers drawing complicated stuff with blue charts, locked up with six to eight men. I was helping with the Balance and Control of the Output. They were prepared to pick my brains and let the men smoke all over me all day. They could smoke all day on Sundays and I thought if you can set fire to the place on Saturday you can equally well set fire to the place on Sunday, it was not logical. There is a lot of amusing crack to tell you about the Factory. The self importance of men with no brains but with no life. I had the key of the x/d/o and left it in another pocket. Then everyone had access to the room anyway, but this gave them heart failure and I asked Dick to send it back registered. The Manager wrote to Dick and made the cheque out to him too enclosing a sheet of paper with signature of the worker. I laffed. I wrote back and said I acknowledge cheque with thanks made out to Captain Nicholson and presumably intended for me. He also said Mrs. Nicholson left a certain amount of clothing behind which will be sent

MUMMY

out Tuesday morning in the B.U. van. Could you beat it, sending out 12 miles with a dirty old overall, wasting time and petrol when the Country is up against it?

He thought I was being petty minded about the smoking but what riled him was I put at the end of the suggestion, 'After all, woman produced man.' The lust for power trying to kill the spirit of life.

She was a brilliant, beautiful woman and very amusing with her friends. She read constantly and had a mind like a steel trap. She taught us many things, especially to be scrupulously honest and considerate. She always found us out if we did anything wrong. Somehow or other the two of us did not get on. I loved her and would have done anything for her to make her happy.

I wrote this letter on April 23rd, 1994, fifteen years after her death:

My Darling Mother,

It is fifteen years since we could talk, but I have been talking to you throughout the years since you died. I know we never really had a relationship to speak of, and I understand your own pain and grief and disappointment and trauma you suffered as a woman, which totally prevented you from being able to love and express your feelings to me. I watched the sorrow and friction in your first marriage; the grief of loss in your second marriage, and your deepening sadness and frustration with yourself in the last marriage, although I know it was a good marriage. I listened to your hatred and bitterness towards my father and took a lot of blame for everything that had gone wrong ever since I was born. I felt guilty and ashamed and responsible for all your sadness.

MUMMY

I watched the fights you had with your mother and I resolved never to let this happen with my daughters. I watched how you fell out with your brother, your sisters-in-law and your whole family of cousins many of whom I only met for the first time at your funeral.

When you died I hoped you would find peace at last but it has taken many years for me to forgive you. But I forgive you now. I understand you and love you as another woman. I wish we could have come together as friends and shared our sorrows and our feelings and our love.

I know we loved one another really, but I couldn't believe it as the feelings were buried too deep to come out. Just a few nights ago I felt her presence, and the next day the radio played the Londonderry Air, one of her favourites. I am peaceful and happy about her now and grateful she was my mother. I wouldn't be who I am if it hadn't been for her.

Her cousin Jim Henry spoke at her funeral in January 1979:

Mary had her standards and I feel now that her tragedy was that so few people in her life matched up to them. If more of us had (but everyone is human!) her life poor dear, could have been a happier one. Still from the last meetings we had it was plain that she had not lost her zest for life entirely, nor her wit. Her beauty was legendary. When I saw General Joe K. just before Christmas he said he thought she was the loveliest girl he had ever seen. She would have been pleased!

God rest her soul, and I pray that the sicknesses and disappointments that came her way in this life will be made up to her now.

CHARLES PLUMB

Charles Plumb was born on December 4, 1905 to Charles and Emma Plumb. His father was the Bishop of St. Andrews; very respectable. My father was quite the opposite. He was bohemian, creative, energetic, cheerful and happy, enormous fun, and very learned and intense about scholarly things. He made me laugh and was a great friend to me. He wasn't always as protective and nurturing as I thought I wanted my father to be. I missed him dreadfully when I was at school, and was constantly disappointed when he could not visit as planned, probably through no fault of his own.

He was a writer, and at his death was working on an opera, *Captain of Sevilla*. I was seventeen when he took me to my first cocktail party given by Roy Campbell, a poet from South Africa. He was the biggest, strongest man I had ever met. He had a beautiful daughter who was a ballerina. Every time I make marmalade I think of him and his poem about Seville oranges being "the apples of the daughters of the evening star"!

It was maddening for Charles to have me as a daughter. He wanted a blue stocking, and I was anything but that. I loved metaphysics—the last thing he was interested in, being an avowed atheist for most of his life. I did not drink and he spent hours at the pub and at parties. "How could any daughter of mine not drink?" he'd say. When we argued he would listen or be pompous, but he never got angry. He married five times and led his wives on a merry dance. The little black devil in him came out, and he behaved like a chauvinist whenever he felt like it.

He edited *Oxford Poetry*, in 1925 with Patrick Monkhouse and in 1926 with W.H. Auden. He was friends with John Betjeman, the Poet Laureate. I have a letter from John Betjeman:

CHARLES PLUMB

29 Radnor Walk,
London S.W.3 4BP
24th July 1975

My dear Charles,

I very much like your translation of Lorca. Having no Spanish I have only been able to read him in English but your San Raphael comes through more than any other I have read.

I found Toronto very Scottish and Scottish Episcopalean as well as Presbyterian. I often think of your father the Bishop of St. Andrew's. And Jack Lynham has married Barbara his secretary, and of Bruno and Gerald Haynes and of other old Rugbeians such as Rupert Brooke, Theodore Wratislaw, and I often see Mrs. David down in Cornwall, the widow of your Headmaster.

I am now in England again after a short tour in Canada. You are brave to live in Mallorca, I would sooner be in the shadow of St. Magnus steeple, Kirkwall. I would like to see you when you come to England. You are a real poet and always have been. I am just a popular success like Tommy Moore and not as good as he and will sooner fade.

Yours ever, John

Charles loved walking and would walk miles for days at a time. His first book was called *Walking in the Grampians*, published in 1935. The first sentence reads "Romance is always around the corner—except in Scotland. There it is in the very air and soil. It is under your feet and in your lungs."

My grandfather died in 1930 so I never met him, and I have very little in the way of letters that would tell me the sort of man he was. Charles mentions him in his book, however, so here is a little bit about Grandpa Plumb:

35

CHARLES PLUMB

From *Walking in the Grampians*:

It was with him that I first climbed Beinn a
Bourd, and of the more distinguished hills it
was the only one which I ever visited in his company; and this has a peculiar significance in my
recherche, because my first recollections of the
hills are linked with him, my pleasantest of him
with them.

I have a natural shrinking from the clerical
collar, whether by aesthetic instinct or associa-
tion—if the latter, it is a fact which the most
casual glance at Freud seems to explain, but
which I prefer to account for by thinking that my
unusual fortune in having known some of those
clergymen, who may be counted amongst the
best and not the worst of mortals, has trained
my eye to see with a painful certainty through
the usual pretensions. Only on holiday—which
meant, in the Highlands—did my father discard
that distasteful adornment, and at least matricu-
lated into the lay world, in a tweed suit of the
profoundest grey. I remember the suit with affection, though I always rather disapproved of it at
the time; it showed up so far on the hillside—as
bad as white. Then he also smoked out of doors,
which he did not at other times; and to this day
the smell of tobacco out of doors, commonplace
for others, retains for me this individual associa-
tion...

The only part of that first Beinn a Bourd day
which I can actually recall is our return over the
top of the Slugain glen, the last look back to the
hill, and the fast last miles home begun, he in his
raven plumage and his fragrant cloud ahead, and
I behind, singing brassy bits of *Tannhauser* at
the top of my voice. It was in a burn a couple of
miles down to the left from here that I bathed,

the last time I was that way, in a patch of sun-shine on a day of storm. What more than leg-endary monster does a man feel himself when running across the windy side of a mountain, naked but for a pair of tremendous boots—too wet already to be worth taking off!

I love that.

My father wrote poetry all his life, both published and unpub-lished. His book *Toward the Sun* was published in 1956, and *The Satires of Juvenal* (verse translation) in 1968. A delightful book of shorter poems called *These* was published in 1970.

Here is one about his beloved Grampians:

MY GRAMPIANS

There is one word in my heart I have never spoken,
Crystal unbroken,
One love obscure from wrongs,
The winters kept it under,
But now is the time of summer, the time of songs.

They lie so guarding my heart I sometimes wonder
Fear doth not plunder
A solace old as theirs,
Shrined like a love-token -
Hills, where the deer and blue shadows are travellers.

☘ ☘ ☘

He wrote this long letter when he was fifteen. (Sorry, I do not have the maps to which he refers):

Fender Cottage, Blair Atholl, Scotland. 24.08.20

Dear Father,

There is really a good deal of news if I remem-ber and inscribe it. Jock arrived on Thursday evening. I arrived JUST in time to meet him after being up Ben-y-Vrackie with Mother. Next day we had the first expedition, up Beinn a'Ghlo.

We started at about ten o'clock, riding (or wheeling) our bikes to Morgie farm. Here we began to walk. We went for four miles over a gradually ascending moor across the front of a ridge of a hill, Carn Liath, the nearest part of B a' G. Having gone right to the left of this, we turned to the right over the edge of its shoulder and round the side of a sort of corrie above the pass between Carn Liath and the opposite nameless part of B a' G. Thence coming up to a bealach, the water-shed of this pass. The other side of this we lunched at a height of nearly three thousand feet. Before this we had only had one short rest. After lunch at about half past two, we went on down the other side of the watershed along another burn for some way till we turned up another pass to the left between 'the nameless' and Carn nan Gabhar, the highest peak.

Carn nan Gabhar is for the top part a very stony and forbidding hill, which had inspired us with awe at lunchtime when we had a glimpse of the near shoulder; it is a long ridge with the highest part furthest north. Turning northwards up the pass, after some way we deliberated about the best ascent. We had meant to go straight on up the pass to the end, round the shoulder to the right and back along the top, for some silly reason labouring under the misapprehension that the top was our end of the ridge in spite of the map, thus:- (a map follows)

Nevertheless in spite of the formidable appearance we decided to attempt to get up the side. So when we had got a long, long way up, not far from the ridge-top, we found ourselves unable to proceed and had to almost come down again to continue along the pass as before

This was a great waste of time and trouble. On reaching the shoulder after some time and meaning to turn to the right as planned, we saw before us what was obviously the actual top. Here the wind was marvellous; we could stand, but more easily fly (only unfortunately in the wrong direction). There had been a good wind below so at 3,500 feet imagine. The top is all stones—you know the way—there are three almost level cairns in a short radius. Behind the highest we rested awhile and admired the view. We saw Lochnagar quite well, but the Cairngorms were mostly in mist. We then returned, keeping along the bottom of the passes by the burns.

I forgot to say that on the way up we found two clumps of white heather close together, one quite a large one. Talking about which, Mother found three lots on Ben-y-Vrackie. We rested again where we had had lunch and then went on over the very extensive moor to the farm. Then on our bikes we slipped down the mile and a half to the cottage and there fed (abundantly). We reckon to have walked at least seventeen miles; we also walked solidly for at least eight hours, allowing generously for rests. (A sketch map follows)

Continued on 26.08.20 (Saturday)

We meant to train to Dalwhinnie and bike back visiting lochs Ericht and Garry. At the station we heard that the train had broken down. Therefore we went to the Pass of Killiecrankie, where we lunched, though driven about by wasps. We visited the Falls of Tummel from this side. Later we went to the Falls of Bruar. We went so many times through the pass that day that we were sick of it. (A map follows)

Shiehallion. Next day we started at about seven for Shiehallion on bikes. The expedition had luckily been pronounced impossible by Mr. Dixon so we were very pleased. Without going right to Kinloch Rannoch we started from a farm called Tenfor, paying toll to come over a bridge! Then we started to walk. There were several parties in the ascendant, but we beat all by a long way by going a much more direct route up though steeper withal. At the top the stoniness is appalling. The walk up is really very little for a hill of three thousand five hundred and forty-seven feet. There were a lot of wasps, and a nest just at the very top. There soon arrived an English (a possibly American, but not very) gentleman, with whom we made friends.

It was a lovely day and we admired the view with the aid of maps. It was a great contrast to Beinn a' Ghlo, for here were people, birds, wasps and flies while there there was nought but a few sheep. Beinn a' Ghlo was as wild as imaginable. The view was excellent; a very fine one of Ben Lawers especially. After this we had lunch and then descended. There are a colossal lot of hares on the hill. We then biked back by Lock Tummel, as I did before. We arrived home just in time for dinner. See map of my previous run. (Map follows)

Next day I somehow did not feel very well, but got up in the afternoon. The Bruces came and had a picnic. In the evening we all went to Songs of the Hebrides (Marjay Kennedy-Fraser and Margaret Kennedy). We all enjoyed it very much. I have heard them at school. I know also you and Mother did at St. Leonards. I had heard one or two but most were new. I wish they had had the harp and Patuffa K.-E.

Next day we tried the Dalwhinnie push again, but going down the hill we had a bike accident. The bike was unfortunately somewhat smashed but not seriously, luckily. My bags were torn open hopelessly, which is sad, as I now have only my green suit to wear. Beyond which a few scratches and bruises were all the harm done. Jock escaped just, and did not come off. So twice the expedition was spoilt. In the afternoon we took the bike to Pitlochry, after I had taken Jock to Old Blair, where Cleverhouse is buried. We had a peaceful evening.

Yesterday, feeling slack, we went into the hills the other side of the Garry by Mrs. Bruce's farm. She insisted on giving us some melon, and lending towels. We had an excellent bathe in a dam there they use for the purpose, they being all out for a picnic in Glen Erochy.

This morning I saw Jock off by the seven o'clock train. I am going to Ardvorlich on Monday, when the others go home. Today we are going with the Bruces to a fete at Forab. I think it will be very nice.

The Bruce's farm is awfully nice; when Margaret stayed there—as she did last week—she slept in a hammock, which considerably elated her. I have seen the same, and it certainly looks very comfortable.

I have decided that "the old lady" is not particularly muddle-headed, but merely possesses an inadequate knowledge of the intricacies of the English tongue. I (at any rate) have enjoyed this holiday very much in spite of anti Blair Athollian prejudices and insanitation.

CHARLES PLUMB

We are all looking forward very much to seeing
you again, and send love,

Your loving son, Theodore

✾ ✾ ✾

Charles wrote this poem to me for my fiftieth birthday:

In the name of Venus, these lines are to bless
your pinnacle of life and loveliness:
Bravely, voluptuously my Queen
Sail on the wings swan-upper never curbed
Forgetting not, yet forego the transitory scene
The trembling arch, the scandal unobserved
(though fluorescent in a modish frame)
No more need you, deluded mortal, claim
To find your god, your god of the embrace,
And turn to find but Vulcan's aluminium face
Wing splendid like a swan over the sky's expanse
To chords like fans or clouds descending to ascend
Wing like those swans of the dark lake of Coole
(Yeats' surf-sail image)
Yours to rule, to make the ocean-lakes of Canada your lake -
Only for one thing, always your one thing, a loving thing
Loving not till death
For death is nothing - better till daybreak
At day-break swan's afield
For Valerie on May 14, 1982 from Charles

He had so much confidence and charisma. I am sure he never
doubted anything he did. He was a great pal as he made me laugh
so much; I felt safe in saying anything to him even if he did not
agree. He never drove a car as he wanted to be able to drink. He
was good at gardening and chopping wood and hopeless about
mechanical things. One day in Mallorca, he let Bill drive down
a mountain round all the hairpin bends on the wrong side of

the road. We were laughing about it later and he said "I thought it was a special way of driving." I envied his optimism. I left the iron on while we were out and it burned a great hole in the kitchen table. "Well at least you didn't burn the house down," he laughed.

There are many letters and parts of letters written by Charles to his parents during those long school years away from home. Here is an early letter from his prep school in Crieff, Scotland written on November 29th, 1914:

> Dear Mother,
>
> It is not long till the Holidays now hurrah! I have not got a war game called 'The Way to Berlin.' Have you got it? It is given with the December number of the Childrens' Magazine. Here is a Latin vocabulary: (He listed thirteen nouns, followed by four French nouns.)
>
> We were all wearing Scottish Lions yesterday, it being Scottish Flag Day. I am as before allways merry and bright.
>
> With tons (16030201) cwts (19) qrs (3), lbs (19), oz (1) of love from Theodore
>
> P.S. Please pretend the letter's longer.
>
> Bit left out.
> I should like my birthday cake to be of white sugar, with a Scottish Lion in the middle, and the Flags of Belgium, France, the Union Jack etc. so as to form nine flags altogether.

In another letter he says "We are all knitting garters and comforters for the soldiers here." His first letter from Rugby School was dated 24th September (probably 1916).

> Dear Mother.
>
> I am quite happy here. At present a lot to do. Am getting into Study 38 soon with a man

called Green. I am in Upper Middle II and No.10 dorm. Trousers must NOT be turned up. VERY important. Mrs. Macintyre, matron, decent. I have seen lots of people. It is very nice just now. I can't find my way about this rabbit warreny School House.

Much love to all, Theodore

Again from Rugby but a few years later in 1920 when he was fifteen:

I don't know how you will take this, but I think that even if you are a bit bored now, you will be glad later.

To you both,

I know Father thinks I spend too much money on myself. I daresay I do. But I don't spend his and ask him for more, do I? I haven't asked for more pocket money from you yet. Also I do not get into debt. If I borrow money it is only when I KNOW I can repay it, and I always do repay it (which is more than lots of men do).

If I spent your money I should try to economize, and in any cases in which I do spend it, I think I try to economize. I am thinking particularly of the hols in all this. I do want to enjoy myself, and I suppose I AM selfish, as you would say, but for fear of hurting my feelings, but I think that if I don't enjoy myself when young, I never shall. In the term I can't, and so what remains but the hols. But I don't mind working in a way that interests me a certain time even in the hols. That is, if I can pay for my pleasures in work. I don't mean school work or anything like it. I think that to make money is better than to save it, and if a reasonable way could be found I would try it. (Not manual, but I don't mean that I wouldn't, take exercise, even violent, so long as it was not a 'show.') If I could help Father in his work it would be excellent. AND I AM SURE I COULD TOO SOMEHOW. I do hope you understand me, though it is very difficult to be lucid.

But then I do want to go to dances and all that kind of thing. I ABSOLUTELY MUST HAVE EVENING DRESS. I don't want you to get me it. If (reckoning, as I suppose I ought not, on five or six quid at Christmas, and the bank) I provided about two-thirds or three quarters, would you give me the rest for a Christmas present?

I am sorry about this, but I cannot bring myself to thinking of going out once without it now. Please understand that I can at least be TREATED as being grown up now, and the outward and visible sign does count for a lot. As to character. You need not bother much, I think, really. I am not really very bad, and though I would not be good, I have a fixed code, which is quite good enough for most people. So there you have it; I don't want to be more than a certain amount good, nor yet more than a certain amount bad. There is however one thing I wish I had told you before. You will be amazed, but I have been smoking a LITTLE, though not very much. (Hols of course.) I am not prepared to stop, that is if you try to make me, but I will tell you how much I do, exactly, if you agree. And this will not be much. There is no harm in it within certain limits. As a matter of fact, I know enormous people who smoke like anything all the time, so it can't stop your growth.

I suppose you will be very bored about this. But I should not have and shall not do it, if I think there is anything wrong in it really. The only thing that worried me was you not know-

CHARLES PLUMB

ing, and I didn't actually dare tell you for fear of your present wrath. You will be glad in the future, you know.

Please see all these views. And I hope we shall get on a bit better than somehow we seem to have been doing. Let's all try too, to right the family fortunes. Cheer up Father! This effort has been rather a strain but I hope it has its effect. I expect scathing answers, at least I don't know. At any rate my equanimity will be helped by not being cock-house." (Meaning "cowardly," I think.)

I can't find the rest of this courageous letter.

After he died, I dreamed I met him on Yonge Street in his blue pyjamas. Delighted, I said, "How did you get here?" "She locked me in my bedroom but I climbed out of the window," said he gleefully with that smirky look I see on the faces of all my babies and grandchildren.

Later I told Lucy, and she said "MUM, we BURIED him in those blue pyjamas." I had no idea.

Once he arrived in Toronto from New York. "How was your trip?" I asked. "There was one SMALL hitch—I went to the wrong airport!"

He was always telling me to stand up straight and put my shoulders back.

He was mugged once in Palma when he was in his seventies. He said to them as he lay on the ground, "You didn't have to knock me down." They apologized after taking his money. "Well, help me up then." He never told them he had more money in his pockets. Someone asked him at a party in Scotland, "Excuse me is your name Pleydell-Bouverie?"; "Yes it is—pronounced Plumb."

My father had a special kind of bloody mindedness unequalled by anyone else I have ever met, except perhaps three people: my son, my grandson, and me!

46

CHARLES PLUMB

In the summer of 1990 he had jaundice. We called often and Peggy assured me he was getting better; there was nothing to worry about and I need not come over. I had planned to go over the following month. (Peggy later admitted she had not wanted to tell me how serious it was because Charles was in the room.)

Lucy decided to fly there the very next day. He died a few days later and here is the conversation they had the day before, on July 16, 1990:

Charles: I'm very unhappy—wish it didn't have to be like this but I guess everybody has to die sometime.

Lucy: I'd rather die quickly like get hit by a car.

Charles: Yes.

Lucy: Do you want to go on living?

Charles: For Peggy. I don't want Peggy to be unhappy.

Lucy: I think it's up to you. Peggy and I have done all we can do and the doctors have done what they can do. I think it's up to you. If you want to live it has to come from your own inner strength, and the strength of your soul; if you want to die then that's OK.

Charles: Yes, the doctor said the analysis will be ready in two weeks.

Lucy: Yes, but you have to decide now what you want. You don't have time to wait for the analysis which may or may not have hope. You decide now.

Charles: Nods his head.

Lucy: Do you believe in reincarnation?

Charles: Yes.

Lucy: What do you think about all these days when you lie so quietly in bed?

Charles: I think about past acquaintances and experiences. (He pauses.) The worst thing about it all is the strain on Peggy.

Lucy: Yes, but I'm here.

Charles: It's so wonderful of you to have come. Peggy and I have talked about my flat, and we have decided that Justin (Juliet's son) would have it... But I think you should have it. Peggy would agree.

47

Lucy: Don't change anything in your will. You've given me everything I want in your poetry.

Charles: You are sweet.

Lucy: I was thinking today that the thing I cherish most in life is the written word... Without it nothing would have any meaning.

Charles: You are good to me.

Lucy: I never realized what a wonderful poet you are until now. *Toward the Sun* was way over my head, and this is the first time I have read *These.*

Charles: I must sign your copy.

Lucy: What about your unpublished poetry? Will Grace handle all that?

Charles: Yes.

Lucy: If she doesn't, I will.

Charles: Valerie and Juliet will have the publishing rights.

Lucy: That's great—I know Mum will be very good at that.

Charles: Valerie and Juliet have always been very good to me— very attentive.

Lucy: Yes, it's hard for them to get over now because they get too busy and have too many responsibilities to take care of—as is life.

The next day July 17, 1990 when Lucy was out buying leeks, he died.

WARTIME

Everything changed in September 1939. We were living in a cottage outside Penselwood, a tiny village in Somerset. One lovely sunny day, Daddy—as we still called him when we were little—came to see us. He explained that he and Mummy had divorced. The bottom dropped out of my world. Furthermore, they were going to send us both away to a boarding school. I could hardly believe it. We had never been to a school except when I was four. I was devastated.

It felt as if everything happened on the same day, but it was all in the same month. They said we were at war with Germany. I went into the garden feeling so sad. I thought it strange that we could have peace and silence—beautiful sunny days with the birds and the bees—and war, all at the same time. Granny was miles away in Ireland and could not comfort me.

A few days later we went to The Knoll School in Kidderminster, Worcestershire. Juliet was only four, and I worried about her as we were in different classes. The day we arrived a boy called Julian came out and shook my hand. I was so impressed I gave the name to Ben as his second name.

I loved being in the first form. We did fractions in Maths, and studied Latin and French, as well as all the other subjects. I took piano lessons, and we played cricket and rounders. The boys were a bit rough, especially in cricket, but the games were super. Our parents sent us postcards and we wrote to them once a week, I felt insecure and sad inside. I had a job to do keeping an eye on Juliet, which helped. Fridays were bad as the weekly boarders went home for the weekend and we never did.

On my ninth birthday nobody sent a cake or a card and the school forgot about it. I was too shy to tell anyone so it was really depressing. I was always in trouble. If Juliet was sent into a corner I argued with the teachers till they punished me as well.

WARTIME

Mummy married Dick Nicholson as soon as the divorce was final. He was a darling and mad about her. He had been a schoolmaster before the war but joined the Army as a Captain in the Leicestershire Regiment. Our only constant home and haven was Granny Gage's house. Dick was kind and gentle with us, but I wished my parents would love each other again. I believed, as children do, that it was entirely my fault they had broken up in the first place. When my mother got angry with me, Dick would calm her down—but she never forgot the times he defended me.

Their daughter, Perdita, was born on September 22, 1941 at Enniskeen (Granny's house) in Newcastle, County Down, during our summer holidays. We were thrilled. She was adorable, calm, and easy for us to look after whenever we got a chance. She had a cleft pallet so could not suck, and had to be fed with a teaspoon. She had a successful operation when she was two.

When I was eleven we left the Knoll School and I went to Sunny Hill Girls' School, in Bruton, Somerset. There was a lot of uproar and argument in the family. The Chancery Court had to be consulted and everyone had to agree. This sort of thing went on all the time.

We lived outside South Brewham in a cottage on top of a steep hill. I went to school on my bike five miles away. Juliet went to the village school until we both became boarders. I cut the grass and chopped wood, and we helped Mummy as much as we could. Dick came to see us whenever he had leave and we had lovely times together. One beautiful day in June 1944 he went back to his regiment. He cycled down the steep hill and up the other side and waved to us when he got to the top, as always. We never saw him again.

Three days later, an idyllic summer's day, the three of us went for a walk. Juliet went home on her bike and I kept walking and walking with Perdie in the stroller. I couldn't go home and felt so sad. I knew what had happened. When we got home poor Mummy had the dreaded telegram. I felt so sorry for her but couldn't say a word. I didn't even cry. She must have thought I was heartless.

50

WARTIME

She went to bed and did not get up for several days. I took care of Perdie carrying her about everywhere. I wanted to protect her and make up for the loss but felt helpless. In the morning my father was there. He had taken a train and walked miles across fields. He stayed to look after us until Mummy could get up again. I was ashamed because I was so glad to see him when Dick had been killed. For months I prayed that Dick had been just wounded and taken prisoner, and would come back to us safe and sound after all. It was hard to believe that such a lovely man could have been killed. Mummy never got over it.

The letter that Granny wrote to Jim Henry (one of Mummy's first cousins) on July 31st 1944, regarding Dick's death, can be found on page 20, in the chapter on Granny Gage.

In a peculiar way the war gave people validation: a reason things were not going well. Everyone had to deal with problems and fears which they kept to themselves. We learned to knit as we had to make scarves and balaclavas for the soldiers and sailors. We were taught to say lots of prayers and to "love the Germans." During school holidays our parents took it in turns to have us, and as they both moved all the time, we rarely went to the same place twice. We loved going to Granny's home in Ireland, where we played in the garden, climbed trees and went to the beach.

At some point Daddy had married a young woman called Dawn. She was blonde and pretty, but we never liked her. She told us not to get up till midday and to stay in our room.

I decided we must try to read the entire Bible as a project. Poor Juliet. We only got to the end of Deuteronomy. We loved being outside all day climbing trees. We met a super fourteen-year-old boy called John Richardson. I had a crush on him and thought I would love him all my life. He was very patient with us. I was at the top of a huge tree one day, when the branch broke off leaving me dangling very high up. John ran down his tree at top speed and up my tree to rescue me. I can see him now.

Dawn was oblivious to us unless she had had too much to drink, when she would wake us up and insist we call her 'Mummy.'

WARTIME

I did it for a quiet life, but Juliet refused and Dawn just would not leave her alone. Charles was in the Home Guard and had to go up to London every night, so he never knew what was going on. Dawn went out a lot to the Canadian Air Force base at Coulsdon. One night there was an air raid while she was out, so we got under the bed and stayed there all night. We were scared of her so we didn't tell anyone; I felt safer when we were alone in the house, air raid or not. She was found out, as her mother and all her sisters arrived early one morning before she got back. There was an almighty row.

The most nerve racking experience during the 'Dawn' era happened one sunny Sunday at Oxford as we waited for a punt on the river. Out of nowhere, a damaged British bomber crashed into the next field. Flames shot sky high and all the bombs began to explode. Everyone rushed towards the fire including my father who asked an old lady to look after us. It was terrifying. I was sure I would never see him again. My feet wanted to run but I could not move. I felt I had turned to stone.

They all came back and took us out in a punt. They gave us Walls ice cream, huge blocks of it. I could not touch it. Walls ice cream always made me feel sick after that. It was so sad. The plane had crashed on a house and the people had all been killed. All afternoon as we drifted on the river, planes flew over dipping in salute to the burning plane.

Very soon Dawn and Charles divorced and she went out of our lives. We heard she died in Calgary while she was still quite young.

Our cousins Jink and Bill Gage, sometimes came to visit when we were at Enniskeen. I was put in charge of Bill who was a sweet little boy, four years old. When I was with Granny I had a sense of belonging, but our visits were much too short. It was sad to leave her to go back to school.

One holiday we were in Hinckley near Coventry. We had to be very careful about the blackout. Homeguards watched the windows and Mummy was always getting into trouble about smok-

WARTIME

ing. She had to smoke in her clothes cupboard. One day I sat on a wall watching lovers hand in hand and realized how lucky I was to be ten and not eighteen. Thousands of young men went off and never came back. Everyone in the country was determined to fight to the death.

Another place we lived was Purley near Croydon, where we heard the sirens more often. Mummy said I had to stay in my room at night, but gave me her blue faced luminous clock to keep me company. The most scary things were the V-2 bombers. They chugged overhead. As long as you could hear them you were fine, but if the noise stopped that was where they dropped. I knew in my heart that God would take care of us.

My mother sent me, by myself, to a lecture on Christian Science. I loved it. She gave me *Science and Health with Key to the Scriptures* by Mary Baker Eddy. I took it back to school and read it at night with my flashlight. It made sense to me.

Many children were sent to other countries where they would be safe and out of the war. My father wanted to send us to cousins in South Africa, but my mother was dead against it.

Here is a letter she wrote:

Dear Charles,

I am afraid I could NEVER agree to sending the children all over the globe. I think these schemes are very wrong, this running away. How can anyone say where people are perfectly safe unless they know of themselves that they have Divine Protection. How do you know that Japan won't start in U.S.A. when they get there. In any emergency in England if the children were with me they would be alright. It is the fear that other people put in them. If you were to tell the children in a bombing raid that it was only fireworks they wouldn't feel a bit frightened. And it is the fear in their hearts of people that ultimately kills. If it is children that Hitler wants it is children

53

he will go after. Surely it is obvious to you that it isn't purely accident that most bombs have fallen in southwest England. If you slap children all together it is a much easier thing to bomb them than if they were scattered about everywhere.

Hitler counts on winning this war by terrorizing people, well he won't kill me that way. They run here they run there and eventually get killed by a motor car. How easy to find out when all these shiploads of children sail and to bomb the lot and I don't think even you then could ever forgive yourself. Personally I think London will escape all bombing. What about the man who evacuated his wife to the Orkney and Shetland, a child was killed a few miles from here evacuated from the East Coast, a woman left Aldershot and went into the country where the house went on fire and one woman was burnt to death.

If you examine yourself honestly you will find that it is only a way of evading your responsibilities and getting rid of them and the children, and presumably when they get to the far corners of the world looked after by God knows who you will say 'well I did it all for the best.' No no a thousand times no. If you leave the children with me in time of danger they will be as safe as I am and I feel very safe because I do know that God does love all those who do trust in Him and believe in His power.

Here is another letter from Mummy written again from Hinckley when we first got there, probably sometime in 1940.

Dear Charles,

Just a line to say the children are very well and very happy here or seem to be. Both very pleased with your postcards today. Your mother I thought looked better than I've ever seen her.

WARTIME

The children like the little house very much. I never wake them up for these air raids and they don't hear them. School does not appear to have changed either child. They will need new coats for the winter term shall I buy them and send you the bill? You could rely on me not to pay very much! When they have gone back I shall knit them some jumpers but have not time just now. Valerie will write. Juliet really cannot write on her own. I find she can't read either. I do still think that school is about 6th class and Valerie has not yet lost her common voice. I think all the people who teach there must have cockney accents. I have had their hair cut and am trying to get it a bit more civilized looking. Valerie has to have an india rubber at her elbow which holds us back rather.

Yours, Mary

It was a relief to go to an all girls' school and not have to contend with the irritating little boys all the time. I still felt terribly shy. But I enjoyed the challenge of the work, especially English and Maths. We kept on knitting for the war. One term Juliet and I had to sleep in a house separate from the school, in a room with a double bed for sisters. Juliet and I fought a lot in this double bed. I was knitting a gigantic grey scarf in the dark for the merchant navy, and she kept snatching it away, causing havoc. I did finish it and wondered who got it in the end. One winter holiday I taught Juliet to knit as we sat inside a snow covered gorse bush.

Sunny Hill was a huge school after the Knoll School. There were playing fields and tennis courts. We played netball and rounders at first, then grass hockey, tennis and cricket. I loved all games and being out in the open air where I could forget my troubles. Sunny Hill School is now known as Bruton School for Girls. It was anything but sunny—actually perishingly cold and windy, being on top of a hill.

55

WARTIME

When I was still a daygirl, Mummy sent me to Bruton to join the Girl Guides. They were very tall and gave me a test. I had to go and see what time it was on the church clock, which meant going through a labyrinth of passages to the market square; I knew by the time I got back that the time would have changed. So I said it is 'about' 4:20. They told me to do it again; I said if they were so keen to know the time they could go themselves. They said I was not fit to be a Girl Guide, and I said I didn't want to be one. My mother looked pleased when I told her.

My mother hired a car and a driver to take us back to school. The smell of leather and cigarette smoke always made me very sick. Juliet got the brunt of it, but she stayed calm and never seemed to mind. I never saw my mother without a cigarette.

Our Head Mistress, Jane Wells, was the reason we were sent to Sunny Hill. She was from Dublin and had been to the same school as Granny and Mummy, the Queen Alexandra School. She had always admired Granny from afar.

Miss Wells said the same prayer every morning, "Help us to grasp the fleeting moment and fill it with purposeful endeavour before it shall pass away into the dim unknown." It is etched into my brain forever. We sat on the floor in straight lines while she scolded us, and told us never to forget that we were the future mothers of Britain!

Miss Wells also came to my rescue many times. Sometimes instructors would send me to her, hoping I would be really punished; but she always said, "What have you done now?" and made me sit down and talk to her. I loved her very much, and she came to my wedding in 1959.

I loved music, though I did not do well with piano lessons. When I would practice at home Mummy would ask how long I would be making that awful noise, so I gave it up. But I loved the choir. We had a wonderful teacher and went to the Bath Festival every year, where we won prizes.

I got confirmed, as my friends were all going to do it. I liked the idea of being "a soldier of Christ" and wearing a veil for the

WARTIME

occasion. The Vicar came to prepare us, and we argued. He said my ideas were heretical. The Bishop of Bath and Wells confirmed us.

My best friend, Anne Ramsden, was an only child and sometimes her parents took me on holiday with them. We laughed all the time. She was very sensible, and became a Prefect and eventually Head Girl. I was proud of her. We are still friends. I broke the rules until the bitter end.

There were two boys' schools in Bruton, but we were forbidden to have any contact with them, so we fantasized about them, calling them silly names.

I thought Gary Cooper was the most wonderful man in the world and Ingrid Bergman was my favourite film star. In her biography her daughters said she never felt sorry for herself— 'she just went on.' She had a vulnerable sweetness I see in my own daughters. She died on August 29 (her own birthday), 1982 at the age of sixty-seven.

When VE Day came I was thirteen. I was balancing on my knees on the end of my iron bed to see how long I could stay there, when someone rushed in with the news. It was very, very, very exciting.

TEENAGE YEARS 1945 - 1949

Mummy found a cottage at Shiplake-on-Thames, near Henley. It was fun being so close to the river. She told us to 'go and find someone to teach you to swim.' We found an old man in Henley called Mr. Parrot. We had to lie across a trestle on the grass to learn how to do breast stroke. Then he tied a long rope (attached to a long pole) round our waists, and walked up and down the river bank while we flailed about in the freezing dark weedy water. We actually learned to swim! We had to take the bus into Shiplake station and the train to Henley. Then we walked all over Henley across the river and a long way down the other side to Mr. Parrot. After that we did all Mummy's shopping in Henley and went home again. When we could swim we were allowed to rent a rowing boat and go out all afternoon. I rowed Juliet. We had no life jackets of course. We rode our bikes and hung around the locks. One good game was going fast down a hill to the river and stopping just before you fell in. Juliet hated it when I made her run along the river through people's gardens. By the time they came out I had disappeared and she got the blame.

We went back to school from Paddington Station in charge of the guard. Old ladies beamed, telling us their schooldays were the happiest days of their lives. I never believed them. We hardly ever saw the guard and had to change trains. We played hop-scotch on dark platforms as huge express trains thundered past.

My mother was very keen on developing initiative. I was twelve when she said I must bicycle to Granny's house near Camberley on the other side of Reading from Shiplake. She gave me a sandwich and a map and told me on no account to go through Reading. I sat on grassy banks daydreaming and didn't meet anyone much on the tiny roads. When I arrived, Granny seemed to be quite worried.

The only birthday I remember at Sunny Hill was my four-teenth. Mummy sent me a delicious cake she had made herself. However, she had iced it all over and sent it before it set, wrapped

TEENAGE YEARS (1945-1949)

tightly in newspaper which was embedded in the icing. The other girls always had perfect birthday cakes. My mother had been to a lot of trouble though, as I found on the only post card I still have from her (although she wrote every week):

> Off to Sheringham tomorrow 12.30 from London, taking all my warmest clothes. Do hope my cake arrives in time had to go to Henley to post it as the PO here shut on Sats and the icing had not hardened. Better write and thank O (her cousin Olivia) for hers.
>
> Love M

I would love to know what has happened to all my friends. Of course I never went back to any reunions but got news from Anne Ramsden. Here are their names and I have photos of them.

Anne Ramsden is now living in Somerset with her second husband and lots of black labrador dogs.

Ruby Cattell, she was the best at maths. I admired her a lot.

Jennifer Cook, Janet Rump, Sally Game, Valerie McGregor, Patsy Longmire, Nina Vaux, Jenny Dunn and Joan Raymond. They were all pretty girls, clever, good at games and laughed a lot. Where are they now?

The best thing that ever happened was on a Sunday when I was pumping water at the well, and Juliet came running, "Daddy is here and he has brought a lady with him." I rushed in and there at the kitchen table was the prettiest lady I had ever seen. She had dark hair and lovely brown eyes and was wearing a cherry red sweater. I loved her on the spot. We just smiled at each other, and I knew we would always be friends. She was Mary Brough, only twenty-four. I was thirteen. She turned out to be the Good Fairy in my life and has rescued me many times. She is one of my dearest friends.

We loved going to stay with them in the school holidays; Mary was patient and made us feel secure. She was the calmest person

59

TEENAGE YEARS (1945-1949)

I had ever met. They lived on the top floor of Hugh Gaitskell's house in Hampstead. Hugh and Charles were old friends having been at the Dragon School in Oxford when they were ten years old. Hugh was Minister of Fuel and Power. It was quite funny when the country was supposed to be saving fuel and power to see the top floor lights left on in Hugh's house after Charles and Mary had gone to work.

We met their interesting friends in Hampstead as we played outside the pubs. The Spaniards at Hampstead Heath was the best. We went to foreign films at the Everyman Cinema. It was a very sophisticated environment and our father decided it was time to call him Charles. We didn't mind. He was not a 'Daddy' sort of father.

We ran wild in London but had to meet one of them for lunch every day. Charles was furious when we spent a whole pound (240 pennies) on the machines at Madame Tussauds. We jumped on and off buses and took the Underground all over the place. We went to news theatres and to almost all the theatres, including Sadlers Wells and Covent Garden. You could get into the gods (the top balcony) for half a crown. One game was to get into opposite ends of the underground train. Every time it stopped we had to run to the next carriage until we met in the middle. The school holidays were the best part of our lives after the war.

I passed all my O levels in 1948 and stayed on for the next two years, which I would need if I went to university. I wanted to go to Oxford but there was a big row about who would pay the fees. Charles said, "What's the point? She'll only get married." I had visions of trying to study and pass exams with all this going on. I knew I would not have any money for expenses, so I gave up the idea of university and left school after one year of A levels.

1949 - 1953

I enrolled in a Commercial course at the Regent Street Polytechnic Institute. Tuition and books were free, as I was under eighteen and living in London. It was a super year, living with Charles and Mary and going to school every day.

We did Elements of English Law, Commerce, Economics, Geography, English, Spanish, German, French, Shorthand and Typing. I loved it and was thrilled to have finished with boarding school.

A scary thing happened in the Underground one day. A man asked me which paper I preferred. I answered politely, and he got into my train, talking all the time. He got out with me at Hampstead and blocked me from leaving the platform. I tried to be calm but trains came and went, leaving me on the empty platform with this man. I carried on an inane conversation praying he would not push me on to the line. Suddenly one of my father's friends came up behind me and swept me away. It took days to get over it. I was sure this horrible man had followed us home.

We met Joan and Bud Smith from Victoria, and thought they were wonderful. They looked like a couple of stars in a romantic movie. Joan was so pretty with her blonde hair, blue eyes and dimples, and Bud the naval officer, so tall and handsome. We thought Canadians must be incredible. They had come to London for three years, so they came over often. Joan's mother Mary Clark (née Cotton Marshall) was Charles' first cousin.

I was beginning to feel more peaceful inside, but it was short-lived. My mother, backed up by Granny, decided I should come and live with her. It meant going to the Court to get permission, and because I was seventeen, the Master in Chancery decided he would talk to me himself.

Here was my chance to open my heart to someone about how I felt about where I lived and why, but I hate to say I did a terrible thing.

1949-1953

I lied to him. When he asked me who I preferred to live with I said my mother. I also had to swear that nobody had tried to influence me. I was terrified my grandmother would stop loving me. I couldn't risk being abandoned by her and I could not tell a soul. I couldn't tell my father or Mary not to worry I didn't mean to reject them in case the Court found out. I had to sacrifice my poor father's feelings to please Granny. Charles was distraught and I heard him crying. The guilt was awful.

So there I was living with my mother in Hammersmith. I went to stay with Granny most weekends and loved that. My first job was in the subscription department at *National Geographic Magazine*. I was secretary to a very bitchy woman called Miss Minich. She used to scream at me, "Miss Plumb, you should be paying us, not us paying you." When I told her she could get someone else and I would stay until they came she said, "No, you show promise."

Life was miserable. I knew I would never be allowed to leave home and share a flat with friends, as we were under the jurisdiction of the Court until we were twenty-one. Mummy said she would never give her permission for me to leave home, and the Court would agree. I was powerless. Sometimes I wanted to jump under a train. Then I couldn't bear to think of how the driver would feel. I joined the Christian Science church near Kensington High Street and went to Sunday school. We had interesting talks there and my teacher, Hilda Roberts, became a good friend. I met George Millar who was twenty and had just finished Sunday School. We spent hours discussing metaphysics, then writing letters when our paths separated. Now he and his wife, Mhora, are two of my closest friends. I went to see Charles and Mary as often as possible.

Once in a while I went out with men. My mother was so scathing about them that I never wanted to see them any more. The only exception was George Millar. She liked him a lot. Hugh Holmes, Uncle Val's son, took me out a few times. He was Legal Adviser to Unilevers and had been Head Boy at Eton, which I found hard to imagine, as he was extremely shy and hard to talk to. All his family were like that. I loved Auntie Gwen, his mother,

62

and had stayed with them when my mother was ill. She was one
of the sweetest people on earth. I liked Uncle Val as he lived in his
own world. He was a well-known Queen's Counsel and went to
the dog races all the time. When we met, we talked about murder
books. Hugh's younger sister, Jane was a lovely lady. She married
Sylvan van de Weyer and they had three sons: Mark, Robert and
Andrew. Hugh and Jane were very fond of each other. Whenever
I go to London I like to see Mark, who came to my wedding when
he was twelve.

On September 14, 1951 I passed my driving test in the middle
of London. Granny had promised she would buy me a car. That
evening I went to Covent Garden with Charles to see a marvellous ballet. We went our separate ways on the Underground. I
noticed a man lighting a cigarette in a doorway, but was dreaming about the ballet and walking on air. I heard running footsteps, and thought someone was hurrying home. More fool me.
He jumped off the hospital wall and grabbed me by the throat. I
was wearing my black shiny raincoat. I had a fleeting vision of
my dead body if I didn't do something. I screamed so loudly I
scared myself; his fingers loosened a little, so I yelled and yelled
and he threw me into someone's rock garden. Ouch. I was furious and kicked out, but he kept coming at me. I went on scream-
ing and kicking till people came running and he ran away. The
police drove me around for two hours trying to find him. My
poor mother was frantic not knowing what had happened.

I went to stay with Granny and was sure I would never
recover. When I told her I was going to leave my job, she said,
"If you leave that job I will not give you a car." I said, "In that case
I will leave it as soon as I can, and I never ever want a car." I was
furious with her and honestly didn't want it any more. Strangely
enough, our relationship went on as usual; we never referred to
it again. She also used to say, "Don't come here with all that stuff
on your face." I would just laugh, "Then you will never see me
Granny."

I got a job I loved with American Certified Public Accountants, Haskins and Sells. There were a dozen accountants with
two of us doing all the secretarial work. I enjoyed working with

1949-1953

figures, and there was plenty of work so I came in early and worked late. This balanced my stressful home life.

I did not know any men except at work. When people asked me for a date they looked sceptical when I said I went to see my grandmother on the weekend. I was nervous and shy. One of the men at work took me to the Mousetrap and said he would like to marry me, but I would have to keep on working. I was astounded.

I met a man in his forties called Bill Adams. He had his own company on the same floor as mine. He drove me to lovely places in the country for lunch. I could talk to him and he didn't make advances. I knew I did not have the emotional stamina to be in a relationship; I just had to keep my head above water until things changed.

PARIS 1953

Freedom at last. This would be the happiest year of my life so far. The Passport Office had files over a foot high. Two weeks before my twenty-first birthday, I begged them to give me my passport. They were delighted to comply, as they were sick of me.

Margaret and Bernard Cook (my aunt and uncle), had kindly invited me to stay with them in Paris for as long as I liked. I loved being with them and had been to stay in Berlin in 1949, when they were there with the British Embassy. Felicity and I had swum every day at the Berlin Olympic Pool. She was only eleven and completely fearless about jumping off the highest diving board. My cousins were younger. David was born in 1934, Felicity in 1938, and Angela in 1945.

I tried to find a job in Paris so I would not have to go back to London. It was impossible to get a work permit, and my French was not good enough to do a job efficiently. I went to cocktail parties every night, and every day I trailed around offices being interviewed entirely in French. Quite soon I met Mr. Oakley, who ran Whinney Murray in Paris. The London firm was Whinney Smith and Whinney (accountants). He was desperate for someone to help out for a short time. He would hand me a pile of letters and say could I deal with them, then occasionally dictate something to the Governor of the Bank of England. He decided, quite suddenly, to move heaven and earth and get me a work permit, on the condition that I stay at least a year and not marry. I looked for a place to live. It was hard to convince Margaret about this; she was more like a sister than an aunt to me, and we were very good friends.

I found an attic at the top of a house near the Buttes de Chaumont Parc in the 19th Arrondissement, on Avenue Secretan. The house belonged to Madame Chiappe, the widow of Monsieur Chiappe who had been the Head of the Prefecture de Police. She had three children, Jean-François who became a well

65

PARIS 1953

known French historian, Marie-Cathérine and Bianca. I still keep in touch with Marie-Cathérine. Jean-François and Bianca have both died.

Madame Chiappe was the most formidable French lady I ever met. She rented a room to me on the seventh floor, 132 stairs up with no elevator. It was wonderful as it had to be important for her to climb up from the first floor to see what I was up to. *"Mademoiselle Valerie un chateau de cinquante chambres ne serait pas assez grande pour vous"* she'd cry.

I had a bed and a huge wardrobe which held everything. The French windows opened up so I could see everything going on in the street. There was a French lavatory on the top floor which I shared with two other people. It was just a big hole in the floor with a tap where I got all my water. I had a jug and bowl and portable bidet in my room, with an electric cooking ring on the floor. I cooked splendid meals in my frying pan and invited people to dinner. The food was so delicious you couldn't go wrong. I got good at crouching.

I seemed to be the only foreigner in the "quartier"; they called me *la petite anglaise.* My special friends were the baker and his wife (Monsieur and Madame Jambin). They eventually moved near Tours, where Bill and I went to visit Madam Jambin after her husband died.

Charles loved it of course. My mother was furious with me for escaping and would not speak or write to me for over a year.

Charles came and we talked and walked in the park, cooked dinners and had a lovely time.

My friend George Millar came over as well. We had kept in touch, writing long letters about metaphysics. Our lives drifted apart. I think he went back to Australia, but in 1963 we were thrilled to find him living in the next town in Germany with his wife, Mhora, and their first baby, Marcus.

No matter what happened it was all worth it to have my freedom. I was no longer sad or depressed. I was gloriously happy.

66

PARIS 1953

I liked my friends at work and still keep in touch with Gisèle Aunay. I explored the whole city and went to art galleries and concerts, including one unforgettable concert given by Edith Piaf. Paris is still 'home.' At lunch I took my French Assimil to the river, and was there when I knew my grandmother had died. I had always been terrified of losing her, but I felt her love for me and was not sad. Two days later I heard she had died at that moment. Now that I am almost the same age she was when she died, I realize it must have broken her heart to see me go. I never thought about how she must have felt. I could tell her everything. She will always be around.

I was content. Young men, especially French men, made me feel uncomfortable. They were certainly romantic and gallant and had a wonderful turn of phrase. My friend Joan Raymond from school was in Paris and had a boyfriend. I was dying to find out about sex. We had lunch and walked for ages but I could never get up the nerve to ask her. This sounds pretty funny in this day and age. Bill Adams in England wrote and said he would like to come and visit me. This might be a great opportunity to find out for myself. He booked us into the Hotel Montaigne, a very grand hotel almost next door to my office on Avenue Montaigne. Several couturières were on this avenue including Christian Dior. We each had a room with a bathroom in between. He took me out to dinner and we had wild boar. In those days I did not drink any alcohol.

Next thing I knew it was morning. I had passed out as soon as I lay down, and there was a very angry man sitting on the end of my bed. I asked him why he hadn't woken me. He predicted I would end up in the gutter, which made me laugh a lot. We stayed friends and it never did go any further. He gave me a lovely amethyst ring which I gave back to him after lunch in Huntingdon when we were standing on the bridge. He hurled the ring into the river where it must be buried in the mud.

I met my dear friend, Gwen Barrows, an American diplomat and writer, who has been close through the years. She lives in New York. Then there was Yanne Vogt, my best French friend. We saw each other often in the restaurant, so I asked the waiter

PARIS 1953

to bring her to my table. My French is not good and I have never heard her speak a word of English, but we were soul mates. I thought she lived with her mother, as she looked so young. She had three children: Michelle my age, then Françoise, and Claude, who was seventeen. Yanne was married (for the second time) to Peter Vogt and expecting a baby, who turned out to be Isabelle. She was a *vendeuse* in Chez Manguin. Peter died, and her beloved Claude, who became a doctor, died a few years ago. She never got over losing him.

One evening I came home exhausted and climbed my 132 stairs, only to find I had left my key in the office. It was a huge sort of jailer's key and the only one in existence. I had to go back on the Métro. Another memorable day was when the Queen was crowned in June 1953. We watched it all from a café.

I met a French businessman in the Golden Arrow dining car who gave some good advice. He said it is not important to marry a wealthy man but it is essential to marry *"un homme qui veut quelque chose."* I felt safer in Paris than I did in London. The men didn't seem to lie in wait and follow you in the same way. Changing trains in the Métro is a nightmare with long walks up and down corridors and endless flights of stairs. That was something I will never want to do again.

There was a funny time with Charles in Passy Station at rush hour. I went through the turnstile, my ticket popped up and let me through. I was almost in the train when the most tremendous commotion broke out. *"Levez le tapis monsieur, le tapis le tapis,"* the crowd screamed. There was Charles completely oblivious that he had stopped the entire mechanism. It was always fun with him in Paris.

1954 - 1959

I visited friends in Ireland and got to know Marcus Baillie Gage in Dublin. He was thirty-seven and a distant cousin. He had a big house in Ballsbridge. I liked his friends, and he wanted to marry me, which I felt would please my grandmother. How naïve. Marcus gave me a family diamond ring, that was so big I felt self-conscious. I wore gloves to hide it. Three weeks before the wedding I realized I was not in love with Marcus and broke it off. I gave him back the ring, and mailed back all the wedding presents. That taught me not to be so impulsive!

While I was in Paris, my mother had married none other than her first cousin, Hugh Holmes. Hugh, the younger by ten years, adored her. They were very happy. They lived in St. Johns Wood, and I was free to pursue my life without reporting to her.

Although I had been happy in Paris, I found a flat in London. I fell in love with John Robertson, in his thirties, who was everything a girl should beware of. He told me he was in the throes of divorce, and I believed him. My mother had always said, "You are the silliest of all silly girls." One day John's wife called me, and we found he had been lying to us both. There was a terrible row, and I broke up with him. It was depressing living in London.

Mary decided to leave Charles and persuaded me to move in with him. I understood how she felt: he was hard to live with if you were his partner.

When Granny had died, she left her house and the contents to my mother. (My mother and her brother had often been at loggerheads: she put everything up for sale by auction, and gave him nothing from the family. He had to go to the auction and buy treasures my mother should have shared with him. Thank goodness I had been far away in Paris!) Granny had left me the portraits of my great-great-great grandparents, Anne and Francis Moule. They had always fascinated me. She also left me five hundred pounds, which was a godsend, as salaries were low. In

69

1954 - 1959

1956, I decided to emigrate to America. I only needed three hundred pounds to do this: two hundred for a visa, and one hundred for a cabin class ticket.

In April 1956 I set sail in the French liner the *S.S. Liberté*. A little voice told me I must be mad, but it was too late to change my mind! My mother was pleased, and actually had flowers delivered to me aboard the boat. Charles was devastated and would not write for ages, saying I had really gone beyond the bounds of civilization this time.

The ship was half empty, so we had first class cabins. I met some young Americans and got talking to Carl Marcus and Tom. In the morning I was seasick. Tom and Carl made me come up on deck. I was very sick and asked them to go away, but Carl wouldn't leave me. He took me to his cabin, which had a porthole, and looked after me. We stayed together the whole trip. Life on board was wonderful. He was very handsome and kind.

It was such a wrench to part with him in New York. I went to Washington, D.C., as my friend Gwen Barrows was there, and found a place to rent near the White House and the World Bank. I got a job in the World Bank and felt at home: interesting people from all over the world worked there. I kept in touch with Carl, who eventually married the nice Jewish girl his parents approved of. Carl introduced me to a friend of his in New York, Harry Reich, who also became a good friend.

My best friends in Washington were Gwen Barrows, Christian Beevor and Diana Farrant. Christian and Diana (both British) worked in the World Bank. We had lots of parties, and one evening we were introduced to Bob Hope at one of his concerts. I went to stay with Diana in New York when she was painting her apartment. We painted late into the night, wearing nothing but a shower cap.

I worked in the Far Eastern Department with another friend, Clara Ledan from Haiti. A year later I moved to New York, and worked for a starchy man on Wall Street who wanted a British secretary as a status symbol.

70

1954 - 1959

I had a terrible summer in New York. I rented a penthouse apartment for July and August, not realizing that the lower building was being renovated. Cockroaches began pouring out of the walls and up the stairs to my penthouse. The owner disappeared to Oshkosh, Wisconsin, and I could not afford to move out. Roaches got into everything, even my bed and my drawers. When I had a shower they rushed down the shower curtain. I called the exterminators so often they laughed and said they could only kill the weak ones. I started to see cockroaches everywhere: in the subway, on tables in restaurants. I was going mad! Now I love the books *archy and mehitabel* and *archy's life of mehitabel* by don marquis. They are about a cockroach who wrote poems on his boss's typewriter at night and had a friend, a cat called Mehitabel. Here is a bit that archy wrote: (from *archy's life of mehitabel*)

one thing the human
bean never seems to
get into it is the
fact that humans
appear just as unnecessary to
cockroaches as cockroaches
do to humans
you would scarcely
call me human
nor am i altogether
cockroach i
conceive it to be my
mission in life to bring
humans and cockroaches
into a better understanding
with each other to
establish some sort of
entente cordialc or
hands across the kitchen sink
arrangement

1954 - 1959

I saw Harry Reich on Sundays, and was getting fond of him. He was seventeen years older than I was though he didn't tell me at the time. He was divorced and not keen to marry again.

When Siegmund Warburg the merchant banker, was in town from London, he employed me weekends to work on his confidential correspondence. He was charming and easy to talk to. When I went shopping he always wanted to see what I had bought. His work was really interesting, and he left me for hours in his hotel to get everything done.

I went to visit Margaret and Bernard in Mexico City for six weeks in October 1958. It was lovely to see the family again. While I was there Juliet had her first baby, Justin, on November 25, 1958. She had married Richard Moyle but I had not been able to afford going home to the wedding.

When I left, Margaret's son, David, took me to the station and saw me off to El Paso. He said, "Oh, you look sad." I never saw him again. A few days later when his parents were on holiday in a remote corner of Mexico, he shot himself in his bedroom. Felicity was in her room next door. David was twenty-four when he died. He had been depressed since his early teens. Margaret never recovered from this terrible shock.

The train took two whole nights and three whole days and went (often backwards) round and round the most lonely and prehistoric mountains I've ever seen. They were sprinkled with white crosses where numerous trains had come to grief.

Harry and I had a passionate reunion in El Paso. The drive to Los Angeles was beautiful. I found an apartment and he stayed with his father. It was early December, and secretarial jobs were impossible to get until the New Year, so I worked selling Fabergé perfume in the May Company. That was pretty memorable, as Fabergé perfume is awful and we were run off our feet.

I got fed up with Harry not making up his mind and went to San Francisco, where I worked for some stockbrokers and did some work for Senator Hubert Humphrey. It was easy to find a job. I just picked an office I liked the look of, walked in and asked

72

1954 - 1959

if they would like me to come and work for them. They were delighted. But I missed Harry, so I went back to Los Angeles and rented a duplex in North Hollywood on North Croft Avenue.

I had met Felix Stone in Mexico. Her husband was now the British Consul in Los Angeles. I wrote from San Francisco:

Dear Mrs. Stone,

I have been in a mad dash for days now—always being whisked around SF to do something—I do like a quiet evening at home and a chance to read and brood... Three of the men (at work) have asked me out. They are the three bachelors, so as well I am leaving as it is a bad plan to go out with people in the office. I met a very amiable Director of something in the Navy on Treasure Island and he is helping in job finding. He has to make a speech in Chicago end of the month and has a speech 44 pages long; he wants it re-edited and cut to half its size and asked me to do it. Am fascinated though it is probably way above my head... Also met a wicked Dutchman I knew in Washington having his shoes shined. He is dying to get back to Holland and I have typed 30 letters for him in exchange for some money and some sheets... He is very wily but good company and we have a lot of mutual friends.

I seem to be shrinking and my clothes are all too long but can't buy more at the moment and anyway I might get fat and besides don't see anything I like. My father just got married to a girl my age—very glamorous I hear. Harry and I had an incredible time visiting our friends and relations, who one and all lived on the edge of a cliff.

The man next door went berserk the other morning at 7:00 am. Poor man, he was shell-shocked, but we weren't to know that. Next thing I knew the alarm clock, the radio and everything he owned were hurled through the window (which was closed), so there were fearful splinterings and crashes. I had to leave so missed the end.

In SF things have come to a standstill and I have been very gloomy for the first time in ages. However, Harry rang up in the middle of the night and we had a long talk, and he is on his way up here. I feel he is just the man, he knows how to cope and keep a firm hand. I pity any man who marries me but am as sure as I can be that it would be a success. Have been a recluse lately and not got mixed up with anybody, sex maniacs or otherwise.

I loved my next job in Los Angeles. I worked for three men at Mutual of New York, an insurance company known as MONY. All the girls looked like film stars, and the men were always joking. I liked figuring out what clients had to pay for their insurance.

Felix Stone was full of energy and ideas. On the day of the 1959 Academy Awards, she discovered that the Canadian Consul (a sixty-five year old bachelor) was attending them by himself. She insisted that he take me. There was no time to buy a dress or get my hair done, and we were sitting in the second row. We were introduced to Shirley MacLaine, Maurice Chevalier and Peter Ustinov, among others. They were easy to talk to. I love Shirley MacLaine.

In the washrooms, later, I listened to them all chatting. I saw Shelley Winters, Jean Simmons and—my favourite—Ingrid Bergman. The Consul and I went on to dine at the Beverly Hills Hotel, where we danced and stared at everyone. Cary Grant was dancing with Kim Novak. Liz Taylor was with Eddie Fisher. David Niven, Dean Martin, Tony Curtis, Janet Leigh and Peter Ustinov were at the next table. That year David Niven and Susie Hayward won the awards for best actor and actress.

1954 - 1959

Jacques Tati got an oscar for *Mon Oncle*. His film, *Monsieur Hulot's Holiday* is my favourite French film. One of my friends at work had been at school with several filmstars and had their autographs. She said she never bothered to get Liz Taylor's because she thought, "She'll never come to anything."

By September 1959 I was getting even more frustrated with Harry. Not only did he not want to marry, he did not want any more children—having lost his son in the divorce. I thought I could change his mind! My father had just married for the fourth time.

This time Charles had married Catherine, the daughter of a Tipperary pig farmer. She preferred to be known as Zelda and was keen to be a belly dancer. She was twenty-seven. They lived in Eastbourne Manor so I booked a passage to visit them, intending to return to Hollywood.

One of my New York friends had come to the USA in a replica of the Mayflower and persuaded me to take the ship's mast back to Plymouth, England. I sailed back to Plymouth, where someone came to pick up the mast. My mother and Hugh met me off the train in London. Mummy shrieked, "You've plucked your eyebrows—you've ruined your only good point!" I said "If that's all I had going for me it won't make any difference."

It was fun being home again, meeting Zelda who was completely scatty. I felt sorry for her: she had no idea how to do anything. I helped her as much as I could and typed for Charles.

Harry called out of the blue, and asked me to marry him. I was thrilled. I booked a passage back in November. Juliet and Richard were in Shrivenham, where Richard was studying at the Royal Military College of Science. I went to stay with them in a cottage in the middle of nowhere. I told her to go to all the cocktail parties and dances at the college, and I would look after Justin, their sweet little twelve-month-old with lovely blue eyes and freckles. I took him for long walks and felt very content.

On Friday, October 30, 1959, I only had two more days left. Richard was taking Juliet into Oxford to have her hair done that

75

afternoon. I was going with them to shop. At the last minute Richard had to take an exam and sent his friend instead. I can still hear his footsteps coming up the garden path. He walked in without knocking, and there was Bill Mair.

I sat in the back of the car and let Juliet do all the talking. Bill's car, a grey Morris Minor, was called 'Sir Thomas Thom.' Bill had bought it in a field for 30 pounds. Weeds grew in the back window and you could see the road under the pedals.

My plan was to vanish into Oxford. Instead, Juliet disappeared, and before I knew it Bill and I were arm-in-arm, talking as if we had always known each other.

We met Juliet for tea, and that evening went to a movie and held hands. It was very romantic, but I still wanted to marry Harry. The funny thing is Bill and I have always talked and talked. To this day if we accidentally get on the telephone we just talk, as if nothing has happened.

I went back to Eastbourne to prepare for my return to Hollywood. Bill came over and proposed to me. I laughed and told him not to ruin his life. He had a bet with his friend Bill Crouch that he would be engaged by his twenty-fifth birthday, November 16. I told him he must go on with his life, and that I had no intention of staying in England. Besides I did not take him seriously. We drove over to Sussex to visit my cousins Ione and Eric Whittome who had a fruit farm in Henfield. I loved them and knew that they would want to meet anyone I was serious about. When I asked Bill jokingly if he could afford to get married he said, "Of course not." He was a Second Lieutenant in the Royal Electrical Mechanical Engineers (REME), studying for his Engineering degree at Shrivenham.

He went back to college, constantly calling me from phone boxes and writing letters. I said, "Please don't call and waste your money. I will come and see Juliet to say goodbye, and I promise I will see you too." I got on the train thinking how I would be clear with him and get him to understand it would not work. He was waiting on the platform at Shrivenham. To my astonishment

1954 - 1959

I jumped off the train, and before he could even say hello, said "Yes, I'll marry you."

Being a true army officer he went straight into action. Single-handedly, he organized the wedding to take place on December 23rd the last day of term when all his friends would be there, and the College would do the catering. My mother gladly paid for everything muttering about how she hoped I would be nice to this "poor unfortunate young man." She had been wailing "what are you waiting for, a knight on a white horse?" Bill did everything. He ordered all the invitations and the flowers. Dressmakers were too busy, so I went up to London and rented a dress from Moss Bros. For six guineas! I had the family veil. He didn't want me to go out of his sight for a day. I trailed behind him telling him he was crazy but he wouldn't listen.

Harry was frantic and I didn't know what to do. Almost every day he called and begged me to come back. He wrote letters and sent telegrams. Bill talked to him, and I wished someone else would sort it out. I felt great love for Harry but I knew that if he let me down again it would break my heart. Besides, I wanted to have children, and couldn't be sure that he would want them too. It was a huge decision. I wanted to BE married but actually doing it scared me.

Bill wrote:

> I hope you're not having to do too many chores darling. In my opinion you should have no work, but should just 'sit on a cushion eating strawberries and cream' every single day of your life. Gosh that would be a boring existence wouldn't it?

Harry wrote long letters from the depths of despair.

> Nothing would have kept me from marrying you this time. It was the first time in my life that I had adjusted myself to the idea of getting married and liking it. I really feel that there will be no other, ever, to take your place. I felt you

1954 - 1959

belonged to me. I loved you in my own way and wanted to take care of you—never felt it before. I had been working hard and had reached an income which would have assured us a comfortable living without worry. That was going to be my surprise to you. To me you were not only my darling but my little one, my wife and all.

Harry had written to Charles as well. Charles had answered and forwarded Harry's letter to me with this angry footnote:

This was obviously written before he got mine. He is quite right to suppose that my having written meant that he could count on me to trust HIM as my future son-in-law. Where would the world be if men switched their loyalties like you. I will not say like women for I suppose there are quite a few women who don't.

This was pretty funny coming from my father, of all people. Talk about the pot calling the kettle black.

Somehow during all my wedding/going back to America preparations I had managed to write my Christmas cards and signed them from Valerie and Harry. I am afraid I just crossed out Harry's name and put Bill's. The day before the wedding I lost my nerve, screamed at Bill and threw wedding presents about; he just took me over to his friends, asked them to give me coffee and went on his way. I had said one condition of marriage was to keep me warm, so he bought me a sheepskin coat.

We met on October 30th and married on December 23rd. Quite a few cousins and friends came down from London. Very noble of them considering the time of year. Even Miss Jane Wells, my headmistress at school, came over from Bath, where she had retired. Eric Whittome gave me away, as Charles had taken Harry's side and was still furious with me

Well yes, I did feel very guilty for doing just that, switching my loyalties. Now, 47 years later, I am glad I did. I am so grateful for the happy marriage that I had while it lasted, and for my

78

1954 - 1959

beloved children and grandchildren who were meant to come into my life. Darling Harry sent me one suitcase of things and incredibly, we kept in touch. Later on Bill and I went to see him on one of our trips and Bill let me stay on for a couple of days. We played tennis and talked. When I divorced he was alone. Had I been alone too, I might have picked up and gone to California to be with him, but Sophie was thirteen, and it would not have been good for her. Someone else moved in with him. When he died of throat cancer in 1989, she wrote pages to me about how he always talked to her about me.

MARRIAGE

After the wedding, we had a lunch party in the college for fifty friends. My mother had put little shoes on the cake because of Harry. Very sweet. I still have them with the letter my cousin, twelve-year-old Mark Van de Weyer, wrote. He thanked my mother for inviting him, then, "I liked the wedding and the reception, but the turkey was best, it was smashing."

We drove to Devon and Cornwall for our honeymoon where we stayed in pubs and drove about in the rain, or walked along freezing, empty beaches. I felt as if I was setting out to sea in a leaky boat. Miss Roberts (my Sunday School teacher) had always told me to be courteous no matter what and to give one hundred percent; very good advice. Bill was interesting and entertaining, never boring. We both liked reading and talked for hours.

His mother had died when he was very small, and his father had left when he was a baby, and not been heard of since. His grandparents had raised him in Newcastle, until his grandmother died when he was fourteen. After that his uncle, Bill Shutt, had taken him to live with him and his wife, Marion, in Plymouth. Marion and I have kept in touch through the years. Bill had started working in Tecalemit when he was sixteen and then had gone to Sandhurst, where he won the Sword of Honour. When I met him he was in the last year of his Engineering degree at the Military College in Shrivenham.

Bill and I stayed in a village where he used to live. He met old cronies at the bar, and I sat upstairs writing thank you letters. We bought a lot of paperback books to keep us happy until we could get 'home' and start playing house.

We had an army 'quarter'—a semi-detached house near the college. Bill studied every evening, and I knitted by the fire. He wanted to have a baby right away. I said we needed time to build our relationship. He kept on, so I ran out and planted rows of tulip bulbs. "Wait till the tulips bloom." I forgot about all that

80

MARRIAGE

of course, until May 1st 1960, when sure enough they came up. Ben was born nine months later in Singapore on February 2nd, 1961.

I was horribly sick for three months. The doctor gave me a prescription for Thalidomide. My intuition made me throw it away. Thank goodness. Bill passed his exams and was posted to Malaya. The Congo crisis had blown up so all the planes were taken for troops, and I had to stay behind. Luckily I flew to Singapore two months before the baby was due.

We went to Kluang, two hours' drive away, but didn't qualify for an army quarter, so we stayed in a rest house while we searched for a place to rent. Snakes terrify me. Tropical heat is brutal with 100 percent humidity. I kept car windows closed, for frear I would run over a snake and it would fly into the car. We had no air conditioning, only fans in the ceilings. We saw a house in an oil palm estate, but a cobra was sitting outside the front door. Eventually we found a house and a darling tortoiseshell cat (I called Mehitabel) came out of the fields each day to sit with me in thunderstorms. She stayed with me for the rest of her life and slept on the end of my bed so I felt safe.

We became good friends with Christine and Peter Duke, also in REME. They had Nigel, aged two. Later they had Lisa, Charlotte (my god-daughter) and Alexander.

Bill was in charge of a REME workshop with the 1st 10th Gurkha Regiment. We moved in a huge convoy to Johore Bahru across the causeway from Singapore, where we rented a modern house. Ben was born in the British Army Hospital. I had seen my doctor while I was pregnant but in the hospital the army midwives took over. They were fierce and competent. But they were scary and yelled at us as they were run off their feet. When I had been in labour for hours I kept pressing the bell. The nurse came and said, "Don't do that I haven't time to be running down to you." When I felt the baby coming I decided to have him without her. She came in at the last moment and yelled at me not to push while she ran about in her high heels.

81

MARRIAGE

Ben was so strong he turned over by himself in the hospital. I had no idea what to do with him when I got home. Bill was grumpy and jealous and unhelpful, and I was scared to fall asleep in case I didn't wake up for him. Breast feeding was agony. There was no one to ask. When he was ten days old Ben got a high fever and was so red I was frantic. I had a fever as well. People told me not to go back to the hospital, where there were too many infections. I prayed. A friend who was a nurse brought a can of Carnation™ milk and gave him a bottle, which saved his life.

He was not cuddly and cried even more when I picked him up; only his father could calm him down. I felt rejected. The relationship with my mother was unresolved. All the old feelings I had with her were reactivated, and I felt useless. Bill went to work, and I sat with Ben feeling miserable, wondering what to fix for dinner. Mehitabel, the cat, decided she was Ben's nanny and bit my ankles if he cried.

The Family Planning clinic opened only every other Friday and for a couple of hours. I never managed to get there and, of course, got pregnant when Ben was four months old. It was more difficult, as I was out of shape and my life apart from motherhood was exhausting. My job was to look after all the soldiers' wives, especially when all the men disappeared into the jungle on manoeuvres. I kept in close touch with them and visited regularly. I had an amah called Ah Eng who lived in, which was a great help except she was sulky and hard to talk to. I took Ben everywhere with me so she could do the housework and cooking. We went swimming in the Naval Officers' pool and sometimes shopping in Singapore. I bought gorgeous materials and put them under Ben's mattress. He smiled sweetly at the customs officers, and they let me through with everything under the sun.

When he was five months old we went to the Cameron Highlands in the north, stopping in Kuala Lumpur on the way. We had to drive for hours, round and round into the mountains, but it was worth it, lovely and cool and wet up there.

I wrote: "Benjamin comes in a push chair and is very good here and much easier to cope with than in the heat; he looks very

MARRIAGE

sweet in his woolly clothes. I got rid of his prickly heat and he looks well and has four huge teeth."

We saw the Cameron Highlands hydro-electricity project that I had worked on while at the World Bank. Bill was allowed to go down in the tunnels. I wrote: "We are having another baby next Feb you will be shocked to hear! Thought I might as well take the plunge and get two over with while I still have my nerve and then they will be close together and company for each other. Benjamin does love children and is good at playing with them, so as he is such a handful anyway another will just manage in his wake! Hope it is a girl as I really don't want to have to keep on having them!"

Our next move was into Singapore, to an apartment on Orchard Road near the Tanglin Club, where we could swim. Lucy was born on March 9th, 1962 at 3:00 a.m. in that same hospital. This time I had a dear nurse who let Bill stay with me the whole time. Again the birth was a bit dramatic. I had told the nurse I didn't want any drug and that she could depend on me to cooperate. Lucy was about to be born when she said "For God's sake don't push whatever you do." She was cutting away. I asked Bill what was happening and he said, "Don't worry." Lucy had the cord all around her neck and was dark blue. She was cuddly and did not cry much. I tried to feed her with no success, so she got Carnation™ milk as well.

I had a lovely amah called Allie. She was marvellous and fun. When we had dinner parties she got her relations to come and help. I made the desserts. Bill was Aide-de-Camp to the Colonel, and his wife (who had no small children), and was always dreaming up schemes that meant a lot of work for me. I had to have, say, thirty people to dinner at the drop of a hat. I was expected to take all this in stride and keep a stiff upper lip like everyone else. Sometimes it was fun but usually exhausting. Allie and I lined up behind each other to change the babies. I could never leave Ben with her so we tackled the shopping first thing. We went to Cold Storage supermarket and the Singapore market. I was always losing him. I tried reins but he went ballistic. We had no car seats in those days so they just bounced about in the back seat.

83

MARRIAGE

The babies were strong and healthy. I gave them food I made based on pablum and never baby food. Water rationing went on for months. From 6:00 a.m. to 6:00 p.m. no water came out of the taps. We filled the bath and saucepans and scooped it out as we needed it. I tried never to leave Allie with both the babies and all the work. She had a day off every week. There wasn't any time to do interesting things though I did fit in a Japanese flower arranging class and sometimes a little tennis at 8:00 a.m. on a grass court. I went to the Christian Science Church across the road and got a lot of church work to do. Other people did as much as I did, and they had even more children, so I thought I should be able to, but it was really too much for me.

When Ben was ten months old I met my great friend Judy Baker in the garden. I had a brown-eyed baby crawling about in the flower beds with the ants, she had a blue-eyed baby the same age sitting sweetly on his mother's knee. She has brown eyes. Geoffrey and Ben are good friends. Her daughter Pamela was born in March 1963 and is my god-daughter.

We had fun playing with the children and when they went to bed we played Scrabble™ and read. There was no television and the radios didn't work. We could not afford ready-made children's clothes, so Bill made up patterns and cut them out, and I sewed all their clothes and sheets and blankets.

When Lucy was three months old and Ben sixteen months we went to Penang on the train. We saw the Bakers in Kuala Lumpur on the way. Bill had picked up a malarial bug in the jungle and sometimes got high fevers. He usually got sick whenever he had time off. We arrived in this ocean paradise with glorious views and sunsets, and he was ill most of the time. I found a nice girl to help me with the children. Luckily there was a pool in the garden as the beach was infested with snakes. There was a sign in the lobby: "If you get bitten by a snake go immediately to the hospital. Try and catch the snake and take it with you." Can you believe it? So much for Penang.

Before we left Singapore in 1963 we bought a huge set of Noritake china. Now forty-four years later I still have it. Not a

84

MARRIAGE

chip. It has been shipped all over the world. I sent half of it to Lucy when I left Toronto. UPS offered to insure it. I said, "Don't bother, you can throw it up in the air and nothing will happen."

We went down to Devon before our next posting. Bill and I were tense, and he drove too fast on those tiny roads with the high hedges. When I asked him to slow down, he said "I know these roads." Next minute we crashed at an unmarked cross road. Luckily we were all fine except Lucy had a cut on her nose. We rented an Alvis car and were going along when I opened my door to close it properly. An Alvis door opens the other way so the wind rushed in, sucking me out. There was nothing I could do. I didn't call Bill as I thought he would lose control and the children would be killed. Just in time Bill grabbed the seat of my pants and pulled me back. We all got on better after that. I am eternally grateful.

We went to live in an army quarter in Bulford (a benighted place) on Salisbury Plain. This time we had a big detached house. The children were two and a half and one and a half so I spent most of the time under the kitchen table mopping up spilled milk. We had dinner parties but small ones. The children had dinner at lunch time and high tea later. They had enormous fights which made me nervous.

A batman came every day to light fires and take care of Bill's shoes and uniform. One batman called Kinley was fun. He had red hair and a spotty face and was not cut out for the army. His sergeant major hated him so sent him to us. He had a used car business he was always dying to get home to. He made tea for me and took Ben to nursery school. When we got everything done we took the children to shop in Salisbury. Once he tried to teach me to change a tire. He sat there smoking, "Women are so cack-handed," he'd laugh. When I visited all the wives he drove, and the children had ice cream while I ran along the block trying to see all these wives. When he wanted time off I persuaded Bill to let him have it. Our dining room was tiny; one day I was squashed up against the sideboard explaining to Kinley about the silver when Ben rushed in. "Have you got a penis?" he demanded. I tried to shut him up and ignore him but he persisted. "Can I

85

MARRIAGE

see it?" Another time a neighbour came to the front door to chat. Suddenly I wanted to check the children upstairs. It was freezing, with a heavy frost outdoors, and the children had vanished. I rushed out and a lady was carrying Lucy and leading Ben still in their pyjamas. She had seen them running hand in hand down the road at top speed. I felt really stupid.

Salisbury Plain is ghastly. You can lean on the wind and it will hold you up. At the station a little old lady said, "My 'usband must 'ave combed England to find this place." We were very close to Stone Henge—another place I am not crazy about. The house was freezing as well. People came down to see us. My father got on well with Ben and slept in his room. They were two of a kind. Kennedy was shot while we were there. Later when Winston Churchill died Ben asked, "Who shot him?" We had television now but not until 5:00 p.m.. Bill made the most marvellous doll's house with electric light and carpets but we had to leave it behind when we moved to Canada. It was a work of art.

Sometimes we had to go to social events in London and leave the children overnight with a batman. They were marvellous with them although they had trouble with Lucy's diapers (with pins of course). We had to go to a huge dinner and dance in the Mansion House and meet the Queen Mother. I found this sort of thing stressful. You had to get there early and never be late, and I worried about everything. We wore long gloves and had to curtsey properly. Once I was there I enjoyed it. I didn't appreciate it at the time, but it was another way of life, that army life. There were no mortgages or taxes to pay. We moved about so much we couldn't get bored.

In July 1965 we went to Detmold in Germany. This time we were with a Cavalry regiment, The Royal Dragoons. Bill went ahead and we followed by train from Liverpool Street to Harwich, where we took the overnight boat to The Hook of Holland. It was quite a scramble to get the children off the boat and on to the train to Germany.

Our house in Detmold was warm and cosy, thank goodness. Ben went to nursery school and Lucy came everywhere with me.

86

MARRIAGE

I was trying to park the car, a 1959 blue Mercedes, in a tiny narrow street. A little voice piped up, "It is too hard for you Mummyy; better leave it for Daddy."

Detmold is a very pretty town quite close to Bielefeld and Bremen. I found George Millar's name in the *Christian Science Journal*. One day we came home and there were George and Mhora, who had come over from Bremen. We visited and spent Christmas together and never lost touch again. They had two little boys: Marcus and Miles, who were younger than Ben and Lucy. Marcus now has a little boy called Spike. Miles lives in Los Angeles and has two little girls, Juliette and Rosetta.

We went on a wonderful camping trip down through Germany, across the border into France and through the Pyrenees into Spain. Bill put his back out and I had to drive through the Pyrenees. All those hairpin bends and amazing views miles below were most exciting. We drove down to Barcelona and stayed a few days with Margaret and Bernard. We came back along the French Riviera and camped in Italy beyond Genoa. We managed to get as far as Milan. We longed to go on to Rome, but it would have been too much with the children, so we went home over the Alps and the Brenner Pass. There was one lovely stop on Lake Como where we camped under a tree covered in ripe figs.

I was getting bored with army life, and worrying about the children's education. I'd have to leave them in boarding schools when the time came. I could NOT do this to them. They needed their own four walls about them no matter how old they were, and they still do.

When I was fifteen I had looked at the map of British Columbia and thought I'd like to live there one day in the "hot dry summers, warm rainy winters." Australia was too far away and the USA would not be fair to Bill, even if we could get in, as I had already lived there. Bill was alarmed at the thought. He was willing to leave the army, work in England for a year first, and then perhaps emigrate. I wanted to leave the army and leave England in one fell swoop. So we did!

Left to right from top: Francis Moule, his wife Anne Watkins, Theresa Cutting, Great Grandfather Gage with Conolly Gage (on donkey), May Gage with tennis racquet, Judge Hugh Holmes, Aubrey Cutting, May Gage

Left to right from top: Felden, May Gage (portrait), Annie Cotton Marshall with daughters Ruth, Joan, and Mary, May Gage, Holmes family, William Gage's memorial tablet, Enniskeen

Holmes family (taken in 1889) left to right from top: William b.1871, May b.1873 d.1953, Great Grandfather Hugh Holmes b.1840 d.1919, Valentine b.1886, Alice b.1880, Great Grandmother Olivia b.March 27, 1843 d.Jan 21, 1901, Violet b.1878, Hugh b.1883, Elsie b.1876

Clockwise from top left: Charles (Theodore) Plumb, Abraham and Mary Plumb, Bishop Charles Plumb, Charles with his father, Abraham Plumb, Valerie, Annie Gage in governess coach, Aunt Armande (nee Gage) playing tennis, William Gage

Left to right from top: Charles, Conolly and Mary, Charles age 11, Charles in his pram, Charles in kilt, Valerie, Charles with his father, May Gage with Mary and Conolly in horsedrawn coach, Valerie and Juliet

Clockwise from top left: Valerie and Juliet, Perdita (baby), Valerie, Little Miss Muffet, Valerie and Juliet, The Bisto Kids, Valerie with doll, Bill and Jink Gage with parents Nancy and Conolly

Bottom, from left: First Eleven, Second Eleven, Sunny Hill School

Clockwise from top left: Charles with parents Emma May and Charles Edward Plumb, Charles with pipe, Valerie, Valerie and mother, Valerie as baby, Conolly Gage, Charles Plumb, May Gage with Mary and Conolly on swing

Left to right from top: Valerie and Juliet with mother, Mary Gage (Mummy), Juliet, Perdita Nicholson, Little Miss Muffet, Perdita, Dick Nicholson, Mary and Valerie in the garden, Valerie and Juliet

Clockwise, from top left: Valerie with Mary Thomas, Valerie age 15, Charles Plumb, Margaret Cook (née Plumb), Bill Mair as a baby, Bill age ten, Bill in uniform, Valerie, Valerie with Harry in California, Valerie with Juliet

Clockwise, from top left: Valerie age 21, Bill at Sandhurst, Valerie on her wedding day, Valerie and Mary admiring the cake, Paris 1954 with Arlette and Gisèle after work, Ben age four months, on the beach with Ben, Valerie the bride

Clockwise, from top left: Valerie age 40 painted by Peggy Farnham, Bill, Juliet with Justin, Valerie, Valerie and Bill in Florida, Bill in canoe

Clockwise, from bottom left: Bill in Malaysia, Bill being presented with the Sword of Honour, March 1957, by H.R.H. The Duke of Gloucester, Bill with Ben, Perdie with Hamish and Toby

Clockwise, from top right: Arriving in Vancouver 1966, Ben and Lucy, Armande Robinson, Valerie and Bill with Ben and Lucy in Vancouver, Ben and Lucy, Sophie age one day old, Ben and Lucy at Point Roberts, Sophie, tea with Molly McGreevy in the Mountains of Mourne

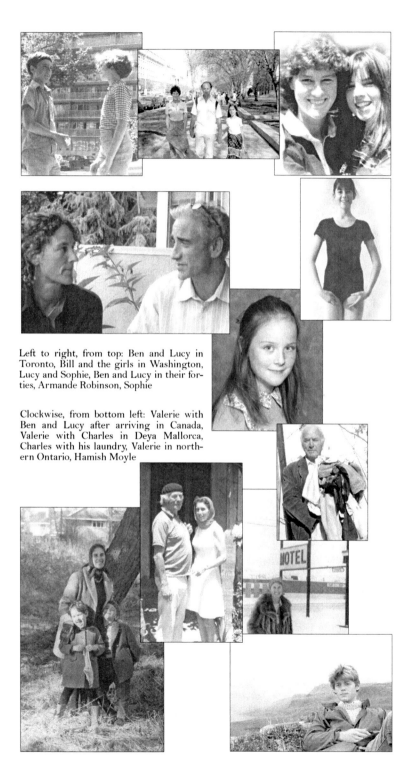

Left to right, from top: Ben and Lucy in Toronto, Bill and the girls in Washington, Lucy and Sophie, Ben and Lucy in their forties, Armande Robinson, Sophie

Clockwise, from bottom left: Valerie with Ben and Lucy after arriving in Canada, Valerie with Charles in Deya Mallorca, Charles with his laundry, Valerie in northern Ontario, Hamish Moyle

Clockwise, from top left: Charles, painted by his wife Peggy Farnham, Valerie with Bill in Montreal, Charles at home in Puerto de Soller, Mallorca, Valerie, Charles, Gillian (Jink) Morris-Adams (née Gage), Jink with Juliet and Bill Gage, Bill Gage, Bill and Valerie's wedding day (December 23, 1959)

Top, from left to right: Juliet with Justin, Hamish and Toby, Valerie with Sophie and Lucy in Toronto, Sophie age six, Hugh Gage and Holly Rowland, Valerie in Vancouver, the children in Toronto, Lucy and Stew's wedding

Bottom, from left to right: Sophie, Valerie with Ben and Sophie in Toronto, the eve of Lucy's wedding with friends Inge Rutgers and Valerie Sloan, with Ben on Valerie's 60th birthday

Clockwise, from top left: Lucy on her wedding day, Diana Gage, Laura Mair, Sophie, Toby Moyle, Valerie with Ben on Lake Ontario, Gage with Gracie, Enshem, 1989 Lucy returns from Israel, Valerie with Lucy in White Rock, Stew with Juliet, Valerie with Laura in Toronto

Top left: James and Hilary Henry (née Holmes) Top right: Tim Gage

Clockwise from middle left: Julie Sabiston (née Clark), Adam and Anne Hogg, Tod and Cathy Morris-Adams, Ben with Gage, on boat left to right: Colin Hempsall, Mary Clark (née Cutting) Ruth Hempsall (née Plumb), Pixie Millar (née Clark)

Clockwise, from top left: Eric Whittome, Ruth and Basil Plumb with Christine (Tink) and Jonas Plumb, Lady Hilary Henry (née Holmes, my mother's first cousin), Jocelyn Valentine (née Hogg, Adam's sister), Valerie with Ruth Plumb, Debbie Morris-Adams, Valerie with Sophie in Mississauga

Left to right, from top left: Kevin Jensen, Sophie, Valerie with Charles in Toronto, Valerie with Mary Clark, Sophie, Mary Thomas, Tim and Diana Gage, Valerie with Conolly Dixon in County Londonderry, Sophie and Trevor on their wedding day in Jamaica, Sophie dancing

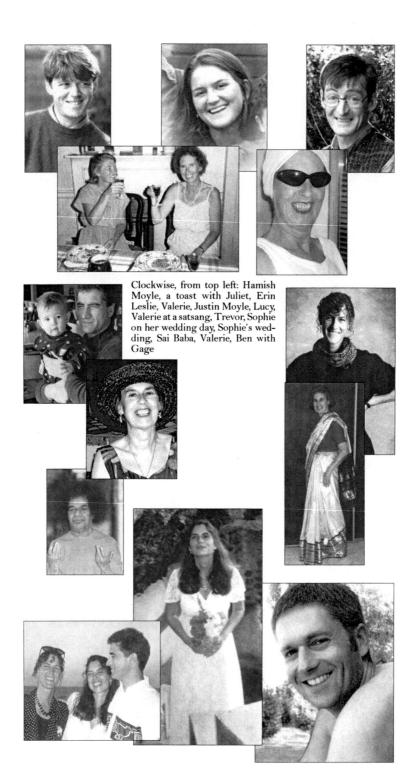

Clockwise, from top left: Hamish Moyle, a toast with Juliet, Erin Leslie, Valerie, Justin Moyle, Lucy, Valerie at a satsang, Trevor, Sophie on her wedding day, Sophie's wedding, Sai Baba, Valerie, Ben with Gage

Clockwise, from bottom left: Valerie with Juliet, Manglam, Jyothi and Danny Singh in White Rock, Valerie with Joan Smith (née Clark), Ben's 40th birthday, Valerie, Lucy, Trevor with Sophie and Laura on Sulphur Mountain, Juliet, Valerie, Laura, Valerie with Juliet in Ireland, Hamish, Justin, Marley and Toby Moyle

Left to right, from top: Hamish at work, Ben and Sophie, Juliet, Ben and Lucy, Valerie, Valerie on Galiano Island, George Millar, Armande Robinson, Lucy with Enshem, Ben with Emma on Vancouver Island, Valerie with Toby in London

Left to right, from top: Emma Mair, Emily Moyle, Emma, Gage Mair, Juliet, Lucy with Diana Gage, Andrew Sosin, Noah Leslie, Ben with Erin, Gracie Sosin, Emma on Vancouver Island

COMING TO CANADA - 1966

We left Detmold and the army on February 28, 1966. When the army comes to 'march you out' you have to go. Jugs, pails, cans of food, gloves, boots, coats, scarves, bags, pillows, rugs, toys, balloons, and half made sandwiches had to be fitted into the car at the last moment. Bill disappeared calling, "There's plenty of room under the seats." I burst into tears, as that's where all my unread *New Yorker* magazines were hidden. We arrived in Dunkirk at 2:00 a.m., exhausted.

March 23rd. We sailed on the *Maasdam*, taking the 1959 Mercedes with us. Bill had tools for everything that could go wrong. I was seasick for three days and worried about icebergs. Ben and Lucy played in the nursery and loved the movie *The Ipcress File.*

March 30. We reached the St. Lawrence Seaway. Tremendous icy mountains to the left, everything blue, sunny and NEW. We had had a great gala night with dinner, dancing and a show put on by the Bluebell Girls (six of the stewards) doing the Can-Can which was hilarious.

March 31. The most exhausting day. At 5:00 a.m. a tugboat was crunching through a tiny channel in the ice. The Customs Office opened at midday. Everyone was hot and cross. There were three flights of non-moving escalators to climb, then down four floors into the main customs hall. Ben and Lucy disappeared into the crowd; we were cleared three hours later. By now they were spitting at a little French boy. No-one looks into 'settlers' effects'; they were more concerned with returning Canadians. While Bill was dealing with customs I found out about car insurance and which road to take. At 4:00 p.m. we stepped into deep mud and sunshine, loaded the car and drove off peering through the stickers on the windshield.

We felt guilty we had no energy to explore Quebec City. There was a gigantic bridge over a huge river. It was exciting to be on our way to Montreal. The General Election results were

110

COMING TO CANADA · 1966

coming in. We had some cheese sandwich biscuits I had bought at the Detmold Naafi for supper and slept at the Cosy Motel in Montreal. Everything needed mending and washing but the *Maasdam* had given us lunch.

April 1st. We left Montreal at 3:00 p.m. after looking up some friends, and reached Ottawa at 6:00 p.m. to stay with my cousins Joan and Bud Smith. Her mother Mary Clark (née Cotton Marshall) in Victoria, had gone to the west coast when she was twenty-two. She told everyone she would not stay she was just going round the world, but she met Cecil Clark and that was that. They had three daughters, Joan, Pixie, and Julie. I was so touched to find a letter from her at Quebec, welcoming us to Canada.

Poor Joan and Bud had written to warn us they were having a dinner party but we never got it. I felt terrible, but they did not seem to mind at all. Their son Julian was eighteen months old and later on they had Sally. We had a lovely weekend together.

Monday, April 4. Fresh sunny day as we drove through fertile farmland. Lunch at Jordi's Continental Restaurant in Deep River. The children had their main meal at lunchtime and a snack before we had dinner. It was a good rolling road and we stayed the night at the Rest Haven Motel outside Sudbury, Ontario, miles from anywhere, where we had delicious take-out chinese food.

Tuesday, April 5. We stopped in Walford at ART's Grill and Diner for breakfast at 10:00 a.m. Art ran the garage and his wife wanted us to stay and work while they had a holiday. We reluctantly turned down the offer! Beyond Sault Ste. Marie it was beautiful going around Lake Superior on mostly dirt road. Then there was a glorious drive through mountains and forests with lakes smothered in deep snow. Side roads were impassable. We drove between high walls of snow for four stretches of 60 kilometres each between gas stations. Nobody at all was on the road. After 440 miles we stopped at Marathon on the Lakehead. Chatted with a Cadbury's salesman who told us moose will charge a train let alone a car, and they are still around. He said when you meet a moose in the road "switch off the headlights and stop, then see who gives in first."

111

COMING TO CANADA - 1966

Wednesday, April 6. SNOW everywhere, but the highway looked passable, so we drove in the middle of the road as we had it to ourselves. Lovely glaciers and ravines around but it was tricky. We skidded a lot but carried on slowly as we would have been stuck till Spring! This was real cowboy and Indian country with names like Dead Horse Creek, Bear Trap Lake, Little Squaw Creek, Wolf River, Dog Tooth Lake, Kicking Horse Creek. We had a scare on a hill slipping and sliding all over the place and managed to get to the top without anyone coming down. Ben and Lucy were worried but I explained we always drive like this in snow. After Port Arthur the road was rough and windy, more like sailing.

Bill looked round when he stopped, and had a fit over the chaos in the car. "Toys everywhere!" he shouted. "And you're not much better!" to me. Very funny as it was the least of our worries. "I REFUSE to go along like a tinker's cart," he went on. If I slowed down slightly to try and keep the car straight he'd say, "Keep up the speed." I only had to drive for two hours a day before lunch. We were amazed we got as far as Kenora that evening. There seemed to be very few PEOPLE in Canada!

Thursday, April 7. We arrived in Winnipeg where the Red River was rising rapidly; we whipped over it before it flooded with only a day or two to spare. We had been hustling along thinking about the Red River because if we were too late, we would have had to stop there, maybe forever. The prairies were more interesting than we expected. Beautiful farmland, wispy woods and lovely prairie grasses. This was the very worst day as none of us felt well, we were not even halfway, and we were sick of driving. Later on there was a fearful roar; the silencer had gone so we pulled in to Elkhorn for repairs. The road was first class and not at all lonely. Arrived in Regina, a really lively town. Bill tied up the exhaust pipe some more with asbestos rope (courtesy of Sgt. Buttolph.)

April 8 - Good Friday. Golden golden prairies and no snow. Saw wild geese and went through Moose Jaw and Swift Current. As the car is loaded to the brim the wheels splay outwards and people laugh at us. Other Mercedes flash their lights. Lunch at

112

COMING TO CANADA - 1966

Medicine Hat. Finished knitting a doll's dress for Lucy. It keeps my mind off the road. We saw a weasel, wild duck, deer and prairie dogs playing. We were happy. CBC had really good programmes. Calgary was like the wild west, very American and energetic.

Saturday, April 9th. Breakfast in Banff. The Rockies are amazing. I don't know how those covered wagons ever got through that wall of rock. We drove in Banff National Park on the excellent roads but it was too early to see black bears. Later we were less enthusiastic. It poured with rain. There were warnings about falling rocks, and the wheels started to vibrate. Suddenly we were in a wonderful Swiss valley with farms and orchards, the first greenery we had seen. Arrived Cache Creek and called my sister, Perdie, who was living in Vancouver but leaving on April 19th. Only two hundred and twenty miles to go.

April 10 - Easter Sunday. Jackass Mountain was really steep and we were on the outside. The Fraser Canyon was nerve racking. There were mountains, rivers, lakes, creeks and canyons, gorges and waterfalls all over the place. We had breakfast at Spencers Bridge and drove in torrential rain to Vancouver arriving at 1.30 p.m. with an awful sense of doom. We wanted to drive on and on forever, and never have to stop and deal with LIFE!

We came all the way from Germany without needing any oil. The car needed a few things like a petrol cap, an exhaust pipe, new windscreen wipers, a parking light bulb, new head lamp, two new tires and that was all.

113

VANCOUVER, BRITISH COLUMBIA

It was one thing arriving in this beautiful city and quite another to start a new life. Our morale was low. We had made a pact to keep going whatever happened, but Bill was very discouraged. Even the National Employment Office man who was supposed to be so supportive to 'Landed Immigrants' was nasty; he wondered why Bill had bothered to come to Canada with the little he had to offer, and told him his introductions were on too high a level.

The children missed all their friends so were thrilled to go to Cypress House School on 16th Avenue and Burrard. Bill got a job in Alcan through an introduction from Joan and Bud. I got a job in the Civil Service Commission for two or three days a week. It was a shock to have to take a driving test. There was a book of rules and 238 questions. It was drizzling but not enough for the windscreen wipers to work properly. We turned into three lanes of charging traffic. The light was red at the top of a hill just as a bus came round a corner and waved me to move over (or else). Pedestrians were all over the road. I was sure I had failed. He gave me a resume of my mistakes in his Rod Steiger voice, "Really, Mrs. May-er going round a corner at 20 mph with no hands on the wheel, changing lanes with that truck about to overtake you, not stopping completely at stop signs," etc. Had I any questions? He suddenly turned into human being and told me to come and get my licence. I asked if he meant it. "Phooey," he beamed.

We lost Ben in Woodward's Department Store. He turned up in the Lost and Found Department quite unperturbed. He had insisted, "My Daddy's got himself lost" and was so pleased when we found ourselves again.

One day Bill had a fever, so I took the children to English Bay, but it started to rain and we drove to Dunbar to look up friends of friends. Across the street there was a house for sale, 4067 West 32nd Avenue half a block from the Endowment Lands. We loved

114

VANCOUVER, BRITISH COLUMBIA

it as it was the only house set back from the road with a lovely plum tree in front. They were asking $13,500 and we had $3,000. I fetched Bill to see it. We offered the full price, subject to seeing it again when he was better, and put down the $3,000. We borrowed $1,000 from the bank. Bill's salary was $600 a month. I bought a car for $100. I went to auctions and furnished the whole house for $400. We met Mavis and Julian Fears, Dianne and Gavin Still from New Zealand, Elizabeth and Michael Dorling from England, and Evelyn and Otto Rulofs who lived on the other side of the lane. Evelyn and Otto still live near me in White Rock.

For the first time in my life I felt I had come home. I would put down roots and live here forever. Or so I thought! I went downtown all the time and parked anywhere I liked. Vancouver was a friendly small town. In the evenings I went to the launderette or to auctions at Love's. We went to Christ Church Cathedral and Ben was in the choir. It was probably the best 'family life' we ever had. In September 1966 the children went to Queen Elizabeth Annex School on Crown Street.

Sometimes we visited Mary and Cecil Clark in Victoria and had tea. Mary's mother, Annie Cutting, was Granny's Plumb's sister. She talked about going 'home' so often that her daughters never really felt they were Canadian. Mary had such style, she was a most beautiful, elegant lady. Once she said out of the blue, "Isn't it wonderful that we can sit here like this and not worry about someone coming up the garden path with a machine gun."

When she was eighty, we were in Butchart Gardens. She scrambled up a steep bank, "It is not enough to be eighty any more. You have to be ninety before anyone takes any notice." She lived to be ninety-four. The last time I saw her, she was laughing and twirling her stick around her head, bubbling with joy as she vanished into her building. There is a little photograph of Mary when she was four on my bedroom wall. The account of Aunt Annie's wedding is in the chapter on the Cutting Family.'

I yearned for another baby. It's funny how it comes over you. You hear little babies crying and want to go and pick them up. The others were not enthusiastic but they had no choice. Sophie

115

VANCOUVER, BRITISH COLUMBIA

arrived on September 17, 1967. I had a lovely time sewing all my own maternity clothes. Lucy and Ben could swim by now. I swam at Spanish Banks the day before Sophie was born in the Grace Hospital. This was the hardest birth experience. They would not let Bill come in. It was a Sunday afternoon so they brought in a group of medical students! They also gave me an epidural against my wishes, so I was cross. My doctor waved forceps around; I told him he had to put them away or I would not cooperate. The students' eyes were popping out of their head. I announced that the only person in the room having a baby was me, I would have it on my terms and they should all back off. Nobody said a word.

I called the baby Juliet Elizabeth. My mother wrote a furious letter saying there would only ever be one Juliet for her and how could I do such a thing. I had written all my birth announcements, and now my mind was a blank when it came to names. When people asked I burst into tears. We only had thirty days to register her name. It took us almost that long to call her Sophie Isabelle Ione. I brought her home and put her on the floor for Ben and Lucy. Ben went and picked her up as if he had picked up tiny babies all his life. She was like Ben, pulling away as he used to, but this time I didn't get upset. When she was fifteen months old she held up her arms to me for the first time. Sometimes I left her in Evelyn's garden across the lane and ran up to Dunbar. Life was pleasant and 'normal'! If that is possible.

Later I met Doreen Bellamy, a kindred spirit, who became one of my best friends. She had Geoffrey, Rod and Lisa. Geoff and Ben were very alike and after school we had chaos with all six children running around. Ben went downtown on the Macdonald bus to choir practice in the Cathedral every week.

There was a holiday for Nancy Greene Day and Ben, now six, was determined to go to the big downtown parade by himself. We had told him he could not do this. He came home for lunch and insisted on going no matter what. I am sorry to say I gave in and took him to the bus. The parade ended at 4oc and there was no sign of him. At 6oc he marched in, "I am late because I was playing in the park." He had seen the whole parade from the front row with everyone giving him treats.

116

VANCOUVER, BRITISH COLUMBIA

I was in the supermarket (now Stongs) on Dunbar with Sophie. It started to rain. A huge black umbrella came across the street weaving through the cars. Ben arrived beaming. "I have come to get you."

I volunteered to work in the Crisis Centre. I interviewed Social agencies about the work they did and wrote articles for the church magazine. One Christmas we filled the house with people and had mulled wine and snacks; people were crushed so tightly we could hardly breathe. I thought the house would fall down.

We rented a beach cottage at Campbell River. Bill and I went fishing, but he left me alone for hours while he went upstream looking for the perfect pool. We went to tea with Roderick Haig-Brown one day. Another time we set out to Whistler. I begged Bill to turn back, as it was too scary. The road was on the edge of a precipice. One weekend we got a baby sitter and went to Pemberton on the train. I imagined a nice little town with cinemas and shops. We got there on Saturday morning. I wore high heels and had a pink umbrella. Everyone stared. There was nothing at all in Pemberton except one hotel. The train was not coming back till Sunday evening. We read every word in the papers and hitchhiked to a river so Bill could fish.

It was heart breaking when Bill got transferred to Alcan's plant in Kingston. I had to have a hysterectomy in September 1969 and was recovering well, but this was a huge setback. We moved in February 1970 in the middle of winter.

KINGSTON, ONTARIO

We bought a pretty house (617 Earl Street) with a white picket fence and everybody settled down happily; all except for me. I missed my friends, especially Doreen. We met Patricia and Gian Frontini, Valerie and John Dalton, and David and Elizabeth Fairbairn, who all had children the same ages as ours.

We went to evening classes where I started pottery. I found a part-time job in the Art History Department of Queen's University and worked with Kay Ferguson who became a good friend. We shared the work for the fourteen professors. I cycled there in ten minutes and it was close to the pottery guild.

We got to know Valerie and Roy Redgrave, a British Army Brigadier, who was doing a course at the Army College in Kingston. Valerie was full of mischief. They came to stay at the cottage (after we left Kingston), and she made me go down the Blue Mountain slide ride; it was terrifying. I visited them when Roy was in charge of the British Forces in Berlin. One wonderful evening we sat in the front row when Herbert von Karajan conducted the Berlin Philharmonic Orchestra playing Beethoven's Pastoral Symphony.

When Ben and Lucy were nine and eight we talked about the sort of mother they might like. Would I be very traditional, or would I discuss everything and be more like a camp counsellor. They loved this idea; Ben said "can we talk about sex now?."

I was painting the picket fence while Lucy and her friends were in the garden. She was the most obedient cooperative little girl. I heard her tell everyone to go home now. They said, "Why should we?." Lucy marched to the gate, "This is my garden and this is my ball."

The winters were awful. I was always backing the car into a snowbank or skidding on ice. One moment I was on the top step, and the next I was at the bottom beside the garbage can.

118

KINGSTON, ONTARIO

You could be walking down the street in your best clothes and suddenly be flat on your back. It was funny at the time, but the novelty soon wore off.

We went to the east coast on camping trips and loved South West Harbour near Bar Harbour in Maine. In 1971 we went to Prince Edward Island and camped at Campeltown on the beach near Souris (mice!). On August 15th I wrote in my diary:

> It started raining and went on all day. Played scrabble with the kids, had breakfast, had lunch, tried fishing and too cold so watched the tuna boat come in and had ice cream. The fishermen said we are in for a bit of a blow. By 6oc the sea was boiling and the wind got up. Hurricane Beth is on its way and we are on the fringes about 50 miles from the eye. I feel I must keep watch and not go to sleep. Am keeping my clothes on. We have to shout over the wind as we dig trenches around the tent and tie the tent and the car to trees. Thought about a tidal wave. Maybe I should watch the sea. The tent is springing the odd leak. The noise is unbelievable almost like the war.

Next day kind farmers came to offer shelter in their homes, but I wanted to stay and see it through. Little trucks were on the beach collecting Irish moss. I hung dirty washing and it washed itself clean. We had dinner out of cans, made hot chocolate and fed the children in the car, as the chocolate blew right out of the cups. I hardly slept that second night either; then it was over. I wrote:

> I was never so glad to see stars in the sky. We cheered ourselves up and bought a teapot and some cigarettes. I needed one. Total rain 42 hours. Hurricane conditions 33.

We picked blueberries on the cliffs after the storm, then played in the huge waves while Bill went fishing.

119

KINGSTON, ONTARIO

South West Harbour in Maine was our favourite place. The sea is too cold for swimming, but there are lovely lakes and woods and we canoed every day. One day Bill insisted we paddle across the lake to get back to our campsite when we could have driven. It was getting rough and people looked horrified as we paddled away.

Doreen went to teach in England for a year and wrote this hilarious letter:

Great to hear from you today. I've been thinking about you too but there just seems to be so much I want to tell you that I'm overwhelmed and can't write at all so hence the air letter. Strangest things keep happening to me here. Don't know if I told you but I had a horrendous accident on January 20 and totalled my car. Had been out for dinner about 25 miles away and was driving home on one of those English winding country lanes—mind miles away, when suddenly headlights from around a bend and a head-on collision. Guess what—I was on the RIGHT side of the road! I leaped out of the car and kept shouting "I'm Canadian, I'm Canadian!" So when the police came they gave me a breathalyzer. He glowered and said, if it turns red, you are under arrest! My God, I stood panic-stricken and watched it go from green to orange and then a thin line of red at the top but it stopped and I passed! No-one hurt to my eternal gratitude. Then I was daydreaming a month later and nearly missed my bus stop—jumped up and raced off and when I got in the flat I realized I'd left my purse on the bus with everything I own, credit cards, the lot. I was in a terrible panic. Phoned bus depot and two hours later a policeman rang my bell and presented me with my bag—intact. BUT—he said "we've met before." It was the same cop who'd charged me in that town 25

120

miles away! I couldn't believe it. So he said, "how long are you staying in England?" I had the feeling he wouldn't relax until I was deported. Then I spent my term break in London as too cold to sightsee and was broke from my Xmas in Ireland with Rod. Decided to go to the Old Bailey and got interested in a case and it was so warm in the court I kept going back every day. One day a young guy came in that looked so much like Rod that I couldn't keep my eyes off him. Finally I got the guy in front of me to tap the young man on the shoulder and when he turned around it really was Rod! I thought he was in Paris but he'd just that week moved to London—10 million people and we end up in the same court room. (Rod is Doreen's son.)

Lucy wrote two poems:

SADNESS

Sadness is when you have to go to the
Bathroom when you are playing a game.
Sadness is not having anything to do or
Not having a friend.

Sadness is when you have to go to bed early.
Sadness is having liver for dinner.
Sadness is having your pet dead.
Sadness is when you go for a long drive in the country.
Sadness is when you hurt yourself.
Sadness is when you have to hurry home
From school because you have to go to
The doctor or dancing lessons or swimming lessons.
Sadness is being late for school.
Sadness is having a hole in your stocking.

KINGSTON, ONTARIO

LOVE

Love is when people care for you.

Love is when someone comes and helps you up

If you have fallen down.

Love is when someone asks you out for lunch or dinner.

Love is when you are all alone trinkling your toes in the river.

Love is when someone comes and plays with you.

Love is when your neighbours love you.

Love is when your favourite TV show is on.

Love is going to the movies.

Love is having your best food for dinner.

Ben wrote a letter:

Dear Mum,

Sorry about bothering you at work about my teeth but the thing that scares me most in the whole world is the dentist. How are you feeling? Did you have a good day at work? From now on you must punish me by taking my pocket money away for a whole month if I don't brush my teeth three times a day. I haven't watched TV at all today. I am very sorry if I have been making a lot of trouble for you this week. Half of my sickness is worries. When I worry I get head-aches and stomachaches like I have right now. Now I'm going to try and write the alphabet with my eyes closed. I won't cheat (he writes it several times.) Now I will try and write a true sentence with my eyes closed. I lobe yui. I lobe you. I love you, I love you. It took me a long time to say it but its true, true and true again. Your'e the BEST mum a child could ever have. You cook much much (13 times) better than the

122

KINGSTON, ONTARIO

best cook in the whole wide world. Everything
I've said in this letter is TRUE.

Love Benjamin (your secret admirer)

Early in 1973 Bill was transferred to Toronto and had to
commute every week. We waited till the school year ended before
moving so that gave me plenty of time to research Toronto from
afar, and decide where to live.

TORONTO, ONTARIO

Bill and Ben were crying as we drove away, but Lucy, Sophie and I were happy. I wondered how on earth I was going to keep three children safe in a huge city. Esther Ritchie next door ran out to give me a tiny fig she had sprouted. It grew into a tall tree and lives with Ben and Laura.

We bought a house at Yonge and St. Clair, 67 Heath Street West, built in 1904. Ben and Lucy had their own rooms and bathroom on the third floor. The basement was perfect for pottery and Bill's workshop. The mutual driveway turned sharply past the neighbours' garage on down to ours. It was quite a feat backing out round that corner. To say nothing of the snow shovelling nightmare. We liked all our neighbours, especially the wonderful Whittingham family with their eccentric dog Barney, a basset hound. He went everywhere in Toronto by himself and all the children in all the schools knew him. We kept each other's keys under our front doormats up and down the street! Those were the days.

I loved the garden, and went with Christian Beevor (now Homsi) to a gardening symposium in Williamsburg, Virginia. Bill did the hard work. One Saturday, there was a huge wedding at the Whittinghams' house. He hacked at a lilac root cursing to himself. People kept coming to use our telephone. I came home on Monday to find tools all over the driveway and Bill had cut through an armoured cable; this started the 'call us before you dig' message on the phone bills. Another time he used the station wagon to pull out a bush and broke the transmission. The car would only go in reverse and we sold it for $75.00. The Queen Mother came to Toronto in June 1973 and we saw her go by. That evening we went to the theatre. I had a brand new Toyota station wagon. Bill sauntered off to the letter box leaving me strapped into the passenger's seat, the motor running and all the beepers going. I barely touched the key and the car took off down the driveway heading for the neighbours' car. I couldn't reach the brake so steered the car into their house, hitting the shingles

TORONTO, ONTARIO

under the dining room. Mercifully they were away. Those houses were so well built there was no damage either to the house or their china cabinet, but the car was crumpled. When we came home it was raining, the lights were flashing, and the horn was beeping.

Bill had no time to explore Toronto with me. There are 296 parks in Toronto, and I must have taken the children to all of them that lonely summer. We joined the Cricket and Skating Club. Lucy and Sophie took skating lessons but soon asked if they could skate in the park instead. We met Maggie and Mark Foster there, and I made friends with Frances Garratt, Lynn Reid and Elizabeth Burridge.

Ben went into grade nine at Upper Canada College, and Lucy and Sophie went to Brown School at Avenue Road. Every November we went to an aluminium convention in either Boca Raton, Florida or Phoenix, Arizona. That's when we became friends with Audrey and Keith Jarvis who live in Etobicoke.

We had a budgie called Louis. He had a heart attack, and after that, his little legs turned all black from the 'knees' down and fell off. We rigged up padded platforms for him to land on and he lived for quite awhile. I grew virginia creeper all over the outside of the house, and filled the house with plants, especially African violets. I worked a shift at the Distress Centre every week for about ten years.

In 1975 we took the children to Mallorca, and stayed in an apartment close to Charles and Peggy. It was wonderful to relax on the beach as the children were older; another time we shared a cottage in the west of Ireland with Juliet and her three boys.

In 1976 Mark and Maggie Foster went to Australia and we bought their cottage in Craigleith. They also bequeathed their little dachshund Shenzi. I thought it would be boring going to the same place all the time, but the cottage was a lot easier than camping. Ben and Lucy loved the RKY camp. Lucy met Stewart Houchen who became one of her best friends, and eighteen years later, her husband. Sophie went to Deer Park School. Her best

125

TORONTO, ONTARIO

friend was Nicol Kalman. Ben did grades nine and ten at Upper Canada. He did grades eleven, twelve and thirteen in two years at North Toronto Collegiate by going to night school as well. Now and again I took Lucy out of school to come with me to the Woodbine horse races.

I loved the cottage, listening to the water, watching the horizon. Georgian Bay is my favourite place. We swam in the icy bay, played tennis and went to the marvellous library. The summers were heaven. We had a canoe and a laser sailing boat. Friends dropped in especially Jock Bennett who became a great friend, and I made cups of tea while everyone sailed out to the horizon. Bill was away almost all the time and Jock was always around. Inevitably he was there for me when things were going wrong and I loved him.

I joined a badminton club in the church on the corner of Heath Street. On Saturdays we always had a long tea break, with cakes and raisin loaf we made. I went there for years even after I had moved away from Heath Street. It certainly beat having to go out in the snow to skate or do cross country skiing. I gave up skating as I kept falling down, but we took the children to High Park for cross country skiing, and I wasn't any better at that.

1979 was the worst year. My mother died in January and I went to her funeral in London. Four years before, I had to accept I would never be able to have the relationship I longed for. I kept in touch with letters and cards. It was good to be with Hugh and my sisters who were devastated. Mary came to the funeral and many cousins whom I only met for the first time. I felt relieved for her that she had gone, as I knew she did not want to go on living. There were so many feelings to sort out.

Divorce:

Bill and I were in limbo, but I was sure it could be solved. Bill's personality changed drastically. He tried to find his father who had left when he was a baby. The Red Cross located him and told Bill that his father did not want to see him. He was shattered. I was sad for him but was no help. We each had to deal with our own demons alone. I wanted to go to a marriage counsellor but

TORONTO, ONTARIO

he would not hear of it. He was offered transfers with Alcan to Brazil and to Australia. I refused absolutely to leave the children while they were still at school, and Bill did not understand.

He wanted to burn his bridges and start a new life. He moved into an apartment and we kept in close touch. He said we would get together again 'down the road.' By December 23rd, our twentieth wedding anniversary it looked hopeless, but I was still sure everything would work out.

Ben went to Guelph University in 1978. He did well and lived with his friend Kerstin Smith. He got a degree in Theoretical Physics. Lucy went to Europe at the end of the school year in 1980. It was really tough for the girls after Bill moved out, and then it was even worse for Sophie as she lost her father and her brother and sister almost all at the same time.

Sophie, Shenzi, and I stayed in the house with all those wretched plants, which took me hours to water and made me furious. I wasn't interested in gardening ever again, and grew ground cover to hide the weeds. I weeded at night before I went to bed to rest my aching back, and bought an electric lawn mower. Sometimes I wished I could come round the corner and find the whole house had burned to the ground. Bill kept turning up. Sophie missed her Dad terribly, but we couldn't talk about it. She started ballet lessons with Marshall Pynkowski and Jeanette Zingg. They are delightful and brilliant. Later they started their own baroque opera company, Opera Atelier. I took their adult ballet class and Sophie got very involved with ballet classes and performances. They were very supportive to Sophie and to me.

The lawyers had warned me that if Bill were transferred out of Canada, he would not have to pay alimony. So I had to agree to the divorce, like it or not. They made me swear not to say a word in court. I went to court on January 12, 1982. Lots of people were there, but I was the only one with two lawyers all dressed up in wigs and gowns. I sat between them doing my knitting. Bill was not there. When it was my turn to go up and stand in front of the judge, he said, "Why do I have to grant a decree nisi here and now?" Bill's lawyer said, "Mr. Mair is going to Malaya. He

127

TORONTO, ONTARIO

wants to get married again and can't take her unless he is free."
This was news to me; I was in shock, but had to be silent. I told
the lawyers off when we got back into the corridor. I managed
to get more than half the house. Bill called, "I did not like what
you did but I admired the way you did it." I said "I had a good
teacher."

A few days later, Sophie was very upset and would not tell
me why. It turned out that Bill got married on January 23rd to
Patricia, eighteen years younger. Ben had been the best man and
Sophie was not invited. On January 24th Bill arrived out of the
blue to ask me if we could always be friends. He was very upset.
I could not believe any of it. How could he pick the 23rd; it was
our date. He said it was the only day the church was free. I said
goodbye, and felt like a mother seeing her son go off to war,
knowing he will never come back.

I woke at nights my head swimming; I was falling into
space. I understood what the 'empty nest' meant; my self-esteem
was zero. The real estate market dropped and nobody wanted
big houses. I took the course in real estate at Ryerson. It was
challenging and cheered me up. Homework kept me busy. I gar-
dened and shovelled snow. My neighbours were a great help. I
met Dwight Williams. We were in the cafeteria so I asked what
course he was doing and he said real estate. I said I was too, and
he said I know, I am in your class. It was so embarrassing that I
hadn't noticed him, I was very sweet and that led to romance. He
was twenty-five and cheered me up. We went to the zoo and he
came to dinner; we did homework together. The girls liked him.
He came from Elliot Lake and had to go back. I drove with him
as far as Parry Sound, intending to take the bus home in time for
dinner. There was no bus until the next day, so I had to call the
girls and explain I was stuck in Parry Sound. Luckily they were
old enough to be left alone. Dwight got married later but we kept
in touch for a long time.

We had five acres of land near Toronto so Bill got that in
the divorce and I got the cottage. Sophie and I loved the summers there. It was always fun to see Jock. He had got divorced.
We played tennis a lot and spent time together. We were good

friends but one weekend he couldn't play tennis and told me he was going to marry a local artist.

The Voice Story:

During the last two years of our marriage, I had had a tightness in my chest but kept quiet about it. My voice would go all funny just when Bill came home. Finally it packed up altogether. It was really hard to speak and my throat was always sore. I saw many doctors. Eventually the University of Toronto diagnosed it as Spastic Dysphonia. There were horribly painful tests in Toronto Western Hospital; weeks later they gave me a botox injection. It traumatized me, it seemed to cut into my soul. It was very new for the doctors and we were their first patients. Of course I never set foot there again. For days I could only whisper, and then my voice improved a bit. It did nothing for my self-esteem. I didn't want to meet people. It was awkward doing business on the telephone. When I moved to British Columbia it was a nightmare as everyone I met was new. It certainly put me off wanting to meet men.

Keath Fraser has written an excellent book called *The Voice Gallery, Travels with a Glass Throat.* There was an article in the *London Evening Standard* about a folk star, Linda Thompson, who found her voice (with botox) after thirty years. When her husband left her, she could not speak for an entire year. Diana Rehm, an American broadcaster, writes exactly how it was with me in her book *Finding My Voice.*

> Spasmodic dysphonia (SD) occurs when the basal ganglia within the brain send an incorrect message to the vocal cord muscles, instructing them to contract too tightly, in some cases blocking speech altogether. Speech may sound strained, quivery, hoarse, jerky, creaky, staccato, or garbled, and can sometimes be very difficult to understand.

> Speaking on a telephone had become a huge obstacle, and this is typical of SD sufferers... I could barely order food at a restaurant, and I was

TORONTO, ONTARIO

embarrassed to try to talk across the table to
dinner companions. What many who experience
SD finally choose is isolation, rather than sub-
jecting themselves to listening to their struggles
to speak.

When she asked her doctor how common a disorder it was,
he acknowledged that there is no accurate data since most people
who suffer the problem are too ashamed to seek help. "For psy-
chological reasons," Dr. Flint said, "many of those who experience spasmodic dysphonia try to avoid situations in which they
have to talk."

This was exactly what was happening to me. I had two
choices. One was to persist with the botox and that was not an
option. The other was to live with the problem and pray it would
get better. I am eternally grateful to my friends who treated me
normally, who never questioned me or gave any advice. If anyone
did tell me I sounded dreadful, I felt like digging a hole and bury-
ing myself. I had to edit what I wanted to say all the time.

I had that dreadful injection in 1993. It was to be another ten
years before I had the courage to get help. Two friends encouraged me to go to Doctor William Morrison at the Vancouver
General Hospital. He gave me a botox injection in February
2003. By then I had been living in White Rock for eight years. It
was a great success. His needles are small and I trust him implic-
itly. It took time to find the right dose for me and now he gives
me the smallest amount mixed with water, about every four to
six months. After the injections the old symptoms return for two
or three weeks, as botox is actually a virus.

I was in turmoil. I sat and watched hockey on Saturday
nights, as that is what we always did. I didn't know what else
to do. Timothy Eaton Church had a lovely dance every Friday
and I went to that. In those days the men were quite polite; I got
to know men I liked enough to see sometimes. Antonio Bibiloni
from Mallorca and Jose Plaza were good friends. They loved to
give advice about money or gardening or cooking. Then they
would warn me about the dangerous men I should be careful of.

130

Pretty funny.

In my craziness I let men I did not love make love to me. They were caring and dull, but they were anchors, and I knitted and watched TV with them. I needed men to find me desirable to feel I was normal. It was tempting to run to Harry in California but I could not uproot Sophie. I took up duplicate bridge. It was easy to get to Audrey Grant's and Kate Buckman's studios. I wasn't that good, but I had to start somewhere, and I went to my badminton club every Saturday.

My cleaning lady Margaret made me laugh. She said "you know Mrs. Mairs, if she ever decides to divorce him he'll have nothing left but his socks." I joined Canada Trust but never liked real estate. When I sold the house, we moved to Don Mills and Sophie was able to stay at North Toronto Collegiate, near Yonge and Eglinton.

Don Mills:

At last, I had my own little townhouse and was much happier. I bought a brand new bed. Sophie had the master bedroom and her own bathroom. We had lots of room and a basement and garage. I felt I was on the dark side of the moon, as I didn't know a soul in Don Mills. I enrolled in two daytime adult courses, Accounting and Phys.Ed. at the high school, where I met lots of kindred spirits, Hilda Downer and Joan Schreiber among others. I joined the tennis club. I took Spanish at night school and met Harry Mannis. He and his wife Elizabeth became two of my dearest friends. They were so kind and invited me over many times. All this time Lucy had been in Israel, living on Kibbutz Lahav in the Negev Desert. We wrote all the time but it was very lonely without her. When she came home I left her with the house, cottage and Sophie, while I went to see Charles and Peggy in Mallorca. Sophie went to visit Bill in Malaya.

I bought a Eurorail pass and spent two days in a charming town, St. Jean de Luz in the south west corner of France. Then I took the train to Barcelona. The train conductor showed me my sleeper and took away my passport. Suddenly, he flung his arms around me. He was so strong I knew I would not be able

TORONTO, ONTARIO

to fight him. I drew myself up tall and said "NO" and he let go as if he had been stung and ran away. There were soldiers with machine guns on the platforms because of the Basque terrorists, so I told them that he had my passport but they said it was the law. I thought about going to Madrid as that train was beside ours, and I had met a group who were on it. They offered me a swiss army knife through the window! The conductor came back bringing fruit and drinks, but I didn't feel safe until a couple arrived with their little boy. We went through dark tunnels in thick fog to cross the border into Spain.

I met Angela and Felicity Cook, my cousins in Barcelona, then caught the ferry to Mallorca. Coming home the train went all round the coast from Barcelona to Marseilles and I visited my friend Christian Homsi in Aix en Provence. After that I took the TGV train to Paris. It goes like a mad thing. It was great to be 'home' again in Paris, but I was very anxious, as I knew trouble was brewing at home.

Lucy met me at the airport with the news she was going to marry her boyfriend Benik Shoshani the following Tuesday. She had met him on the kibbutz and he had been staying while I was away. I was furious with her. Ben was in California and Bill and Sophie were in Malaya. Benik had a nice face and he reminded Lucy to be polite to me. He said it was not 'a marriage for mothers' it was for him to get into Canada. I ranted and raved the whole weekend and on Tuesday they got married in City Hall. I brought our dear friend Mabel Mitchell who used to be a nanny in Damascus, and we got dressed up in hats and gloves. I cried all the way through. Nanny whispered "not now dear." Benik wore his jeans and Lucy wore one of my old sundresses. I asked about the ring and she said "oh we never thought of that", so I lent her one. I took them to our favourite chinese restaurant in Kensington Market. When we got home I went to the tennis club. Next thing Lucy was behind me asking to play tennis.

Nanny was a marvellous character from the old school. She had been nanny to cousins of George Homsi, who married my friend Christian Beevor. They asked me to look her up when I got to Toronto. Some of the things she said were priceless:

132

TORONTO, ONTARIO

"It's all sex sex sex sex, and these little prams on the bus, you're afraid of your feet."

"There's a way of being nasty and nice at the same time"

"You'll have to make allowances for ALL that." (darkly)

"I used to ride horses like nobody's business— over the jumps my Dad made me go. I wanted to be a policewoman in the slums of London." (Her father was a sergeant major with a cavalry regiment in India.)

"God love her, you never can tell."

"Don't pressure him just let him come to his senses. Half a loaf is better than none. You've got to hold a candle to the devil."

"Make the most of your life as later on it's too late, and you'll wonder why you didn't do it. Say your prayers and everything will be all right."

Lucy went to Guelph University and Benik got a job there. I breathed again. They got a letter from Sydney. I sent it on thinking they had friends in Nova Scotia. Before I knew it, they were packing up to go to Sydney, Australia, and I was in an even worse state. I couldn't bear to lose Lucy again. They worked on a rice farm for a few months then went back to the kibbutz. We kept in close touch. She lost her landed immigrant status and had to apply all over again. I went there for three weeks one year, and we had a great time. But I always missed her terribly. She was in charge of the orchards and was fluent in Hebrew. One day she called, "Do you mind if I break up with Benik?" She stayed in touch with his parents Dodik and Zehavka. They are lovely and came to Canada and stayed with me.

Sophie did very well at school and took Russian in grade thirteen. She went to Europe with Nicol for a year. I was having coffee in the sun telling myself I could relax as I had nothing to worry about, when I got a call from a nice lady at the birth control centre asking for Sophie; I had no idea she was going there. They had a great time in Europe as they had lots of friends and relations to visit, but when they came home Sophie was distraught to find her boyfriend Geoff, had found someone else. She took Hotel Management at Ryerson and came to the pool one afternoon: "I can do more with my life by taking risks and chances than staying in school." She dropped out of Ryerson and went on to become a successful business woman in advertising. Ben graduated from Guelph and had a good job with Intel. He and Kerstin bought a house near Eglinton and Jane. They were going to get married but broke up. I invited twelve people to lunch one Sunday, and Bill called out of the blue. He said his aunt and uncle (Marion and Bill Shutt) had come to stay from England but Trish (his wife) did not want to have them, so could he bring them to stay with me. They arrived for lunch and everyone was astonished. I told him I had given him ten extra years of life, at least, as he never had to deal with any of his children's problems. He told me Trish had thrown him out as well. Next day he rushed back to her, and I had a lovely ten days with Marion and Bill.

Ben met Laura Leslie in 1985. In 1989 Ben took her to Jamaica and called to say they were getting married in the morning, but not to try and call back. Lucy and I looked at each other: "Do you feel like the two ugly sisters!" However, they had a wonderful party in their garden when they got back.

Laura has a daughter, Erin, born in 1976. She has always been delightful. Once she said to me, "Well you must have done something right because I always trust Ben no matter what happens." She now has a little boy Noah, born in 2005.

In 1986 I sold the cottage; what a relief. I loved it but it was falling apart. I brought up gabions and everyone helped to fill them with rocks to save it from being washed away. The door would never shut properly so I put Bill's huge sneakers outside to scare burglars.

I found an ideal job, working part-time in Leaside for Alan Zeegen, a Structural Engineer. His wife Saskia worked there too. I arrived in mid-morning, did all the work, and went home before

TORONTO, ONTARIO

rush-hour. I had a little business, Valmair Enterprises, which included making pottery and secretarial services. There was a meditation group run by three young men at the east end of Lawrence Avenue. I got to know Gerry and Harriet Fine there. One evening they showed us a video of Sri Sathya Sai Baba and told us that once you hear of him he will come into your life. Since then he has been a guiding presence. I have written about him in another chapter.

Lucy came home from Israel in 1989. It was unbelievable. Benik came over and brought her beloved dog Enshem. He just walked in after that incredible journey and knew he was home. It was wonderful to have Lucy back after all those years. Harry died later that year of throat cancer, aged 74.

Charles died unexpectedly in July 1990. Lucy came home one day and said she was going to Mallorca the next day. I thought she was mad. Charles had not been feeling well, but Peggy had assured me he was fine, and the doctors had said there was nothing to worry about. I had planned a visit in a couple of months. It was wonderful Lucy was there, as a few days later he died. They talked the day before, and I have included their conversation in the chapter about him. Peggy admitted later she had lied about his illness because he was listening. Two years before, he had been ill and mentioned Teilhard de Chardin. I said, "When you go can you manage to come back and see me." He said he had not worked out quite how to do that yet. Since then he seems to be around. When the radio plays Wagner I turn it up for him.

Sophie and I often went to the National Ballet. She was twelve when we saw Romeo and Juliet. As they danced the bedroom scene, Sophie said in a loud whisper, "I can't see you and Dad doing that."

I saw a lot of Jose Plaza who gave me plenty of heartache. He went off to Spain for weeks at a time, and I stupidly waited for him to come back. My mother was probably laughing from heaven, "I always told you you were silly!" Dr. Brian Bustard was a marvellous help, and I went to him for six years. He always said, "What you see is what you get," when we talked about men.

135

TORONTO, ONTARIO

The widow of one of the Governors General was interviewed on TV. I'll always remember her saying: "You have got to learn to jump the fences because the next fence will be even higher."

Mississauga:

Lucy lived with John Stephens in Newmarket where they had horses. They worked together doing commercial photography. Sophie had moved in with Trevor Sosin and I was free to go wherever I pleased. I bought a townhouse in Mississauga just beyond the west end of Toronto. Alan did not want me to leave, and said I was mad to sell my house in such a bad market. I said, "Sometimes you have to appear to lose in order to gain." I actually made $50,000 on the move. Saskia had become impossible to work with. Alan said, "Why don't you do what I do and ignore her?" They later divorced.

I loved Mississauga and the ethnic shops. The tennis club was very friendly. They had round robins in the evenings. I made many new friends there and at the satsangs for Sai Baba. Jean, Claire and Jen Corinthios, Liz, Greg and Victoria Byfield and Karuna, Vina and Indira were good fun. I wished we had come to live there when we first moved to Toronto. Antonio Perez and Elizabeth MacLean valiantly drove from Don Mills to have picnics.

I met a widower, Lou Bonomolo, and his son Gil, aged 25. Lou and Gil started a tool and die business and let me have a room for my pottery studio. I helped out by taking care of their accounts. The next few years were stressful. Big companies did not seem to care about paying in full, debts piled up, and nothing worked out the way it was supposed to. Lou is a genius when it comes to making machines work, and people needed his expertise, but were not willing to pay.

I learned all I ever wanted to know about business but never dared to ask! This quotation from John Bingham makes me think of Lou although he is Brazilian and French, not an Arab:

Nobody understands the mind of an Arab—

136

TORONTO, ONTARIO

God didn't mean us to, so we might as well stop trying. It's not just money with them, there's poetry comes into it, and real religion, and gentleness and ruthlessness, and wild rages, and love and generosity inside hard bargaining, and simplicity and cunning—and just to make it easier, there's Arabs and Arabs.

In 1992 Ben and Laura gave a huge party for my sixtieth birthday. All my friends came; they even had fireworks in the garden. Two months later they had Gage, my first grandchild. He was a gorgeous baby, exactly like Ben.

Brian Bustard's wife gave a vegetarian cooking course where I met Kevin Jensen who was twenty-eight. We became good friends over the years and only saw each other now and again as our lives were very different. He was a very sensitive gentle soul. He bought a house with his friend Rob, but they fell out when Rob's girlfriend moved in. He wrote:

> He has a better heart than his fiancé, she is very vengeful and cruel and self-centred and I believe a bad influence on him. When Nini (psychic) talked about this situation, she said that I wasn't strong enough emotionally for revenge at this time. She could see their harmful intent. It made me wonder about the connection between revenge and karma. I thought that people's bad deeds would be karmically taken care of, that maybe revenge was creating bad karma for the person originally wronged. I'd like to ask Nini about that. What do you think? I'd be interested in your thoughts. Not that I'm planning anything at all. I always had a feeling that it wasn't quite right. Must be the Christian influence on me. If anyone hurt you, I would certainly feel like getting revenge. So many questions in life, eh Val? You are my best friend, Val, now and always. Hugs and kisses from your Mississauga buddy. Talk to you soon. Love Kevin.

TORONTO, ONTARIO

In November 1993, Sophie and Trevor got married in Negril, Jamaica, where Ben and Laura had married. They wanted their best friends and Ben, Laura, Lucy, me and Trevor's sister Stephanie, to be there. We rented a villa for ten days and had a lot of fun. The wedding was in the garden on November 17th. After dinner we all went to Peewee's bar next door, and Sophie, Lucy and I danced on the bar. It was wild.

That December, Lucy left John and drove west with Enshem and her close friend Val Sloan. She found a job and a place to live in Calgary. I was driving about 50 kilometres a day. It was very time-consuming, and in winter the weather was so bad it was hard to see friends. I knew it was time to go back to the west coast, where I had always wanted to live. I made huge lists of what I planned to be doing in the next place wherever that was, and wrote out affirmations, like 'Obstacles to my success are being removed.' People assured me that if I went west the children would follow. Lucy encouraged me to follow my heart. It was too stressful at the factory; I was getting alarming chest pains. If I had known I would be giving up pottery altogether, I would never have left. I sold all my tools, my kiln and books, but kept the Princess wheel.

It was sad to leave everyone but I knew I was about to disappear without trace, both physically and emotionally, if I stayed. I gave away silver, china and crystal to anyone who wanted it. Toronto had become too much to handle.

Two quotations sum up my feelings for the creative process:

> Shoji Hamada told Tom Marsh that 'No significant pot could be made apart from one's living...' and, therefore, I should not expect my work to be of great importance until my life was what I wanted my work to be.'

And from *The Unknown Craftsman* by Soetsu Yanagi:

> The precise and perfect carries no overtones, admits no freedom; the perfect is static and regulated, cold and hard. We in our own human

TORONTO, ONTARIO

imperfections are repelled by the perfect since everything is apparent from the start and there is no suggestion of the infinite. Beauty must have some room, must be associated with freedom. Freedom indeed, is beauty. The love of the irregular is a sign of the basic quest for freedom.

This sums up how I felt about my work. Or rather my struggle for beauty. Even though I never came up to my own expectations, it does not matter at all, I learned so much from the process. The lessons go on forever.

Dan Millman in his *Sacred Journey of the Peaceful Warrior*, writes about a photographer, Sei Fujimoto. His first love was photography. He practised for thirty years accumulating a treasury of inspired photographs, until a fire destroyed all the photographs he had taken and all the negatives and most of his equipment. He mourned this loss,

> But more than that, he understood the bigger picture, and came to a growing realization that something of great value remained that was never touched by the fire: Fuji had learned to see life in a different way. Every day, when he got up, he saw a world of light and shadow, shapes and textures—a world of beauty and harmony and balance. When he shared this insight with me, Dan, he was so happy! His realization mirrors that of the Zen masters who share with their students that all paths, all activities—professions, sports, arts, crafts—serve as a means of internal development, merely a boat to get across the river. Once you get across, you no longer need the boat.

On March 15 1995 when the movers (Lamb Movers of Richmond Hill) arrived, my neighbour asked where I was going to live. I said I had no idea. She said "I can't believe you would do that." I booked to fly the next day and look around. I would find a

TORONTO, ONTARIO

place as soon as I got to British Columbia and move in by the end of March. That was the plan!

BACK TO BRITISH COLUMBIA

Next day, I flew to Vancouver to stay with Doreen. I went to Coquitlam, Surrey, Ladner, and White Rock on the bus. I loved White Rock the best and it has the best bus service to Vancouver. It was a shock to find I had exchanged one urban sprawl for another urban sprawl.

As soon as I arrived in White Rock one of the buildings seemed to reach out to me. I nearly bought a condo there but the price was too high. The pool was closed, people were on strike, it was not the time to decide. I went back to Toronto for part of the summer, rented a cottage in Thornbury and visited friends. In August I went to house-sit in Victoria for my cousin Joan, and look after her cat. I explored the city, played bridge and went swimming.

My goal was to be settled by September 15 1995, so I went back to White Rock for a couple of days. I bought the condo I had seen in March from Millie and Ed Henderson, who moved next door to me and became my friends. The closing date was September 15, 1995.

Driving was strange after Toronto. You never knew what people were going to do. Winking green lights do not mean it is OK to turn left in front of the traffic! I never found a pottery studio. By the time I got into the tennis club I had not played for two years and was hopeless. I longed for rain, so I would not have to go there. My voice was a big problem. People could not understand me. I was nervous about asking for directions. I missed the children and all my friends. I had had all sorts of ideas about working or starting a business, and learning new things like spinning and weaving. But the energy was not there. This beach is one of the best in the whole world. But I felt bereft.

I went to England in April 1996. My sister Perdie had been diagnosed with multiple sclerosis when she was only twenty-seven. She went to holistic doctors and never wanted to talk

141

BACK TO BRITISH COLUMBIA

about it. She married Vernon Robinson and they had a daughter, Armande. Perdie made light of her problems but it was sad to see her becoming crippled. She kept quiet about a lump in her breast for three years. Up until the end she kept her incredible sense of humour. She always looked young and pretty and had a lovely light in her eyes. I loved the way when something went wrong she would mutter, "Oh bother."

When I went over she was in the hospice most of the time. Vernon had abandoned her in her darkest hour. Armande was very brave and calm. Perdie was unique. There was never anybody like her. When I had to leave I knew I would never see her again. We only had another hour together, the two of us. There were things we might have said, but one of her friends dropped in and did not go. Leaving her was dreadful. We understood each other so well. She was my first baby. She was fifty-four when she died in June 1996.

Emma Mair, Ben and Laura's little daughter, was born on July 6, 1996. Everyone was thrilled. I went back to Toronto to see her.

Nobody talks about the emotional upheaval of having grandchildren. They are attached to your psyche but yet they are not your own children, so there is a great gap there; then our own children grow into adults with their own problems, and there is another gap there. I often dream about my children when they were little again and I like that. My doctor said to me, "The business of having children (she has three) never changes; i.e. I am better off here not worrying quite so much, and if, as one fantasizes, they were actually living here, I would not be seeing much more of them, as I would not be able to do what they were doing or keep up with them. Their attitudes are coloured by their environment, their peer group and their partners. They are not FREE yet to be the people they are meant to be." Thank you Doctor Anna Chlebak.

In January 1998 I went to India from London with a group of British people I had never met. We went to Sai Baba's ashram in Puttaparthi, a three hour drive from Bangalore. It was so moving

142

BACK TO BRITISH COLUMBIA

and wonderful that I have written about it separately in the chapter about Sai Baba.

When I got back Bill wrote to say he could no longer pay me alimony. He moved to the States. It was a nightmare finding a lawyer and waiting for divorce papers to arrive from Toronto. I stopped shopping and going to restaurants. I made my own cards, read, knitted, and sorted out cupboards. There was plenty to do.

It was hard to keep in touch with Ben and Sophie. They must have felt I had abandoned them. One year I went back for Christmas and everything blew up. Snow was falling. I told Ben how I felt, and he listened. It struck me as the first time a man had paid attention and not walked away. It was a very healing experience. Another day, Sophie and I went to Tim Horton's and talked. We would have yelled, but it was Tim Horton's. Sophie said, "Well you are the mother." I said we should talk at least once a week. "Every week!" said Sophie. Now she calls me almost every day.

Lucy's marriage to Stewart Houchen in 1998 was so much fun. Stewart had been her best friend through thick and thin. At last he told her how much he loved her. He left his job in Toronto late in 1997. They were married on July 4, 1998 in Banff, on the top of Sulphur Mountain. Ben, Laura, Sophie and Trevor came from Toronto. Friends came from all over the place. Lucy had Val Sloan (who lived in Boulder, Colorado), Inge Rutgers (from Holland) and Sophie as her bridesmaids.

We woke up to pouring rain; Lucy was ecstatic. She and I and Enshem drove to Banff and went up in the gondola, then finished the long climb to the top. The clouds and mist cleared, and the sun came out. Lucy wore her wedding dress and went barefoot. Enshem had the rings on his collar. It was so touching when Stew, who doesn't show his feelings easily, shouted into the valley "Eighteen years! Eighteen years, I have waited for this moment."

Lucy had made sandwiches and served them in the parking lot before thirty of us drove to Radium Hot Springs for three

143

BACK TO BRITISH COLUMBIA

days, to stay at Addison Bungalows. Lucy had prepared everything for dinner and friends had made the cakes. We had a party
for three days. Inge wrote me a beautiful letter:

> Small details are popping up in my mind! You,
> sitting on your hotel bed, that Friday before the
> wedding. Embracing me like I was your lost
> child! The warmth I felt was indescribable. The
> moment we came up after being at that crowded
> bar and Jonathan was sleeping in your bed and you
> came to sit outside with all of us. The moment
> before the wedding when we were standing on
> top of that mountain, with you, Lucy, Sophie,
> Val, Jonathan (her little boy) and me. When all
> the guests were all ready to leave the cabins in
> the morning, standing at the parking lot and the
> enormous sadness I felt within you!
>
> The hot springs in the evening. When we were
> sitting outside at night with the moon right
> above us. You talking about your children being
> small and you being a mom at that time. The day
> we spent at the beach and you talked to Kather-
> ine about her life and her husband to become.
>
> So many little details that can fill up a book! I
> am so very happy that I met you, so happy that
> you have found peace and wisdom in life. This
> is what is glowing in your eyes. I am happy that
> Lucy has you as a mother!

All this time Kevin had been a loyal friend. We talked every
week. The telephone company has my undying gratitude: during
those awful years I was able to call anywhere in Canada at certain
times for twenty dollars a month. Kevin came to stay with me
and see his B.C. cousins as well. He went skiing at Whistler and
said he would love to come and live in B.C. I was worried; there
seemed to be so much negativity in his life. He was unhappy with
his life and it seemed he was in danger of being sucked into a
vortex.

144

BACK TO BRITISH COLUMBIA

He called me late on September 30th, 2000 when I was out, and I called him back early the 1st October but just missed him. Later that day his mother called me to tell me he had been hit by a car on his motorcycle and was in a coma in St. Mike's Hospital. She said, "You know Valerie he had just bought a ticket to come and see you next Friday, he was so excited." I wanted to fly to Toronto but I had never met his parents. I waited and prayed. Gloria called again and said they had taken him off life support. I felt Kevin's presence very strongly and knew he did not want me to go to Toronto.

Since then he has been a guardian angel. It was very touching that Ben and Sophie wanted to go to his funeral. After the funeral Ben called me on his cell phone and said, "You know Mum I always thought Kevin was really weird because he liked to hang out with you, but he was a really nice regular guy." Ben makes me laugh. Gloria and I keep in touch.

I wrote:

> My darling Kevin—it is November 4th 2000, I am sorry I have taken so long to write and tell you how much I treasure your life and thank you for coming into my life and being part of it for eight years. Thank you for your tenderness and understanding and love and respect and fun and support and friendship and sympathy and gentleness.

> You are my soulmate and I feel you close by. I would have liked to be more deeply in your physical life but I did not want to intrude on your destiny as I saw it—to marry and have kids, all that. So I stepped back from a deeper intimacy, though on one level we had that, and really we had it on all levels, but neither of us wanted to acknowledge that. You were the best lover I ever had as I have told you before and I rejoice in that. Before you left on October 1st when you went into a coma, we had discussed your coming here

145

BACK TO BRITISH COLUMBIA

and I had told you you were in a shift—I never realized how huge that was. I almost tried to discourage you from coming, as I did not want to be trying to influence you to do something I really wanted in case you were disappointed later.

You played the drums, you rode your motor bike—you loved little kids and animals—you were so balanced—the perfect man in my view. I remember the things you said before you came here—when I apologized for not encouraging you one hundred percent you said, "Nothing you do could ever upset me." You spoke with such love and compassion. I could not tell you my fear of not coming up to expectation, or if I did, of not being able to maintain my health and looks and energy. All that week before you went, Lucy and I talked about you—I was playing the tape you made me of all my records that you made for me with such love—I see all the presents you have given me, your photos your letters and cards. I remember when you were going out with Tara how you said so vehemently, "Nobody can ever take ME away from YOU," and you meant it.

You thought you were skinny—you were tall and light footed—I never heard you coming along you would just appear—Your silken hair so soft and that impish grin—I see and feel them now. You will soar with the eagles and show yourself to me in so many ways—you knew I loved you, wanted you and was waiting for you. I always felt I would lose you but I have not lost you—you are closer to me now even more than before.

Lynn said to me, "Rejoice you gave him himself—he found himself with you. You gave him so much—you meant so much to him. Your love was a higher love than we can imagine." I knew

146

BACK TO BRITISH COLUMBIA

that however our relationship went we would be there for each other all our lives. And now I know you always will be. You are totally unique and I am privileged to have met you and to have been your friend on this earth.

Vedic Seers say, "The real you cannot be squeezed into the volume of a body or the span of a lifetime." Gary Zukov says, "You came as a great soul to us to give us gifts and you left VOLUNTARILY."

Darling Kevin, Go to your Destiny.

The NDP government was a great help. My wonderful lawyer, whose name I will not mention, moved mountains. The result was the agency in Victoria that deals with spousal financial affairs made sure Bill settled with me. Ben was extremely helpful in negotiating a settlement with his dad.

My right eye developed a cataract, for which I had an operation in February 2002. My vision started to blur, and there were times when I could not see at all for a few hours. It was all a great mystery, and went on for months. I got a second opinion that was so alarming, that when I went to England a week later I found a wonderful doctor in Moorfields Eye Hospital who agreed to operate. She put in tubes for glaucoma in May 2004. I took a long time to heal but that operation changed my life. I never thought I would have to have eye drops and live my life according to my eyes. I now have a very special eye doctor in Vancouver. Every day I am especially thankful for my sight.

Lucy, Sophie and Ben are my greatest friends. Lucy and I play tennis at the club and love the people there. It was one of the hardest tests of my life to get the courage to go there. Now I wouldn't be without it. Everyone in the knitting group is unique. They laugh a lot and are very caring. The pool is my salvation, so is the bridge club where I play with my friend Frances Gunn. Yoga is one of my favourite activities. Tanesa my teacher is a great friend. There never would have been time or energy for pottery as well.

147

BACK TO BRITISH COLUMBIA

On August 30th, 2002, Sophie's wish came true, and Grace Taylor May was born in Women's College Hospital in Toronto. I went and stayed with her. On September 26th, 2004, Andrew Carter Thomas came along and I went there again. It is sad they are all so far away. I do get back to visit and vice versa and sometimes we go on holiday together.

LUCY - POETRY

DREAM - OCTOBER 18, 1986

In my sleep I saw you sitting there
In the shallows of murky waters
Weeds grew about like forgotten dreams
Wilting in the deadened sunlight.
You refused what I longed to offer
Cutting me deep without a word
Eyes penetrating, hiding your hurt,
Still, not a word, you turned.
Now I gaze upon that still lake
Reflecting memories I always keep
Of a love once lost in waters so deep.

❉❉❉

FEBRUARY 1986

Can't you see you are losing me?
Can't you see the nothingness?
Don't you feel the emptiness?
It's blinding you, it's breaking me.

Your love for me runs so deep
My love for you is running slow.
I'm caught in the river of your love
Swimming, struggling against the flow.
Your love is cruel, your love is blind,
I'm drowning and you leave me behind.

LUCY - POETRY

July 10, 1984

You can lie down beside me
But don't say a word
For the silence will soothe me
With your sonnet unheard
I'd rather not speak
Not see and not hear
Than grow to be weak
From the love I don't hear

✿ ✿ ✿

Here are three beautiful poems Lucy wrote to me:

May 14, 1989 - For Mum

Your world is a temperamental sea
And you are a rock upon its shore.
Standing firm, yet spirit free
The look in your eye
Says you've been here before.

Many a ship has crossed your path
Seeking your guidance in times of wrath.
And many a tide has swept your feet
Pulling and tugging in sullen defeat.

For there is no force
You cannot withstand,
As the strongest force
Is your embrace with the land.

Each new wave that is thrown your way
Tests your strength and ability
Breaking over your back in rippling array
Enhancing your beauty and eternity.

150

LUCY - POETRY

Life's fragile shadow before the storm
Rides in on a wave and kisses your face.
Unbroken by your solid form
Enraptures, enriches, bestows you with grace.

※ ※ ※

May 14, 1991

I've loved you,
From the moment you had me
I've needed you,
From the moment you held me
You are my shelter,
My strength,
My survival.

In my world of the woods,
Dark, forbidding, - unknown,
You've been the sunlight
Toward which I've grown.

In this land of rock,
Which shouts hardship and gloom,
You've been the earth,
From which I bloom.

Love you forever, Lucy

※ ※ ※

May 14, 1992 - For mum

Let's welcome this day,
This 14th of May
In your 60th year,
My mother, my dear,
My friend,

151

LUCY - POETRY

My fate,
My Soul Mate.

I love you to death,
Your voice and your breath,
Your laughter and tears,
Your fun and your fears.

I came to you,
Halfway through -
When you were only thirty.
Your love was my shield -
Your wisdom would wield -
Against all that could hurt me.
Now that I am thirty too -
I want to be just like you...
I want to hold your hand...
Forever.

I want to touch each face
With the same charm and grace
That makes you my idol -
My life's embrace,
My spirit, my soul,
Forever.

There are only three,
As lucky as me -
To have your love through eternity.

I love you Mum -
And couldn't imagine the world
Without you !!!

HAPPY BIRTHDAY!
With love Lucy

SOPHIE

I kept some letters from Sophie; first something from kindergarten:

THE TEACHER AND THE BOY (TYPED)

I am sophie mair and I am here to tell you about the time in school when a boy was shoting spit balls and the teacher came in. well was she mad she said tommy go out in the hall but tommy didn't go he just sat there stund and didn't move a mucle but the teacher didn't know that he was out in space and thout he was disobaying her and she got really mad she nearly broke the whole school down including the pupils. The principle came running the cartackers came running and all the other teachers came running to and all of the pulips came running to. And you know what that mean old teacher was fired for making all that noise. And that is the story of the teacher and the boy.

WHEN I WAS LITTLE

When I was little my belly button kept popping out. Now the first time it happened my parents were really surprised and thought I was having a heart attack. But soon they realized that whenever I cried it popped out. My brother and sister loved watching it popping out. But soon my Dad got tired of pushing it in. My Mum took me the next week to the hospital. Then in the hospital all I can remember is when I was just going into the operating room and it never popped out again.

She had a hernia and had it fixed in Kingston when she was two. She was so brave. She said, "Sorry I have to cry, but it hurts so much."

SOPHIE

Here is a poem:

The stars up in the sky are the lights of the angels houses,

My love is true

And yours is too.

When we love each other

Our souls do not depart.

When our eye has a hurting tear

That mean's evil is near.

God has sent his angel through.

To bless your cold and sickness too.

God will look after YOU

From old till new.

※※※

Sophie's teenage years were something else. Bill and I broke up when she was only twelve. It was a very bad time for her. Ben was away at Guelph University; Lucy was about to leave school and go round the world. Sophie's generation was different from theirs. She had a lovely circle of friends at North Toronto Collegiate. When we moved to Don Mills she stayed there, and met her friends at Summerhill where Nicol lived, and where my clothes finally ended up. Mothers called asking if I had seen brand new towels they had just bought, things like that. They always bought the same dress each in a different colour so they could pass them around. Sophie's bedroom was smothered in clothes, wet towels, plates and books the whole time. I had Mollie Maid to clean and told them to ignore her room.

HERE ARE SOME OF OUR CONVERSATIONS:

Me: I am annoyed you took my blouse.

Sophie: I had it????? What blouse? I might have tried it on. Cheer up—she says.

SOPHIE

Sophie calls me at 7.45 a.m:

Sophie: It's Sophie.

Me: Good God where ARE you.

Sophie: I am at Dave's. I didn't want you to worry.

Me: I'm not worried I'm still in bed. I thought you were home.

Sophie: Would you have worried?

Me: Well you told me not to wake you up so I probably wouldn't have come upstairs. Who is Dave?

Sophie: Well Dave, from BEFORE.

Watching Oprah::

    She is watching Oprah Winfrey. "Why I am Ashamed of my Parents" is the subject, and a girl is going on about her childhood. I try to say something; her hand comes up. "Wait," she says "for the commercial." I wait. In the commercial I say, "I hope you're not ashamed of YOUR parents." "Well my childhood was certainly FAR from perfect."

Watching tennis:

Me: Those two black girls are doing really well.

Sophie: I can't stand prejudice in my own MOTHER.

I return from a trip and find dead flowers after two weeks:

Sophie: I thought you might still want them!

In general:

Sophie: "I'll be home later" she announces. This could mean three minutes or three hours, or three weeks or even three years later.

SOPHIE

Watching senior citizens running:

Me: I don't want to get like that—all spindley.

Sophie: You're already all spindley.

I was typing an essay for Sophie. It took over three hours, with her leaning over me cursing to herself, smoking, changing things. If I had to work for her I could work for anyone. I corrected spelling and she shrieked she didn't trust me and it looked retarded. I was erasing something and she said, "You are shaking. Why are you shaking?"

On telephone to her friend Alison:

Sophie: Did you find anything to eat?

Alison: Chicken (she says chewing).

Sophie: Cooked?

Alison: Mm.

Sophie: Are you eating it?

Alison: Mm.

Sophie: Is it good?

Teenagers:

Carolina borrowed a sweater from Tom, and Francie took it from Carolina's house. Francie gave it to Kim to give back to Carolina. Kim's sister took it from Kim and wore it and now she doesn't know where it is; probably at one of Kim's sister's friends. Carolina is mad at Kim because Tom keeps asking for his sweater.

Teenagers

So confident she takes me by the hand and marches me into the middle of Yonge Street.

SOPHIE

Teenagers:

She leaves. It is 9:00 a.m. She picks her way over the ice. She is wearing a COTTON skirt, a cotton jean jacket, tiny pointed shoes, no coat and no hat. She was home the day before with a cold. I SHIVER.

Teenagers:

Five girls are chirping happily upstairs while we play bridge on a snowy winter night. They saunter past at 11.40 p.m. and wander into a blinding snowstorm. "We're going to the pub now."

Teenagers:

Her friends are all going away to university. They troop in to look for their clothes, upstairs. They come down looking disappointed.

"Is there anywhere else they could be, like any place in the ENTIRE city?"

"Did you look under the bed?" I asked.

"It was SCARY, but we did."

November 23, 1988. We are sitting in a coffee shop on Bayview Avenue discussing her wedding:

Me: Don't spend $1000 on a dress you'll never wear again. Choose one you can go on wearing.

Sophie: Why not, I'll keep it and give it to my children.

Me: Ha ha, believe me they'll laugh they won't want it. (How could she be so naive?) And besides you'll probably have boys.

Sophie: BOYS, I don't want boys. Anyway I want to keep my dress forever even if I don't wear it.

Me: Of course you could always get buried in it!

SOPHIE

September 28 1990 in the Fern Resort one weekend:

Sophie: I just hope I never have a kid like me. I don't know how
you put up with me. Didn't you get worried when I
didn't call and didn't come home?

🔱

She wrote to me from Malaysia when she was staying with
Bill and his new wife when she was nearly sixteen:

Malaysia is the same a bit boring but it's relax-
ing. I've been doing my exercise every day and
am trying to lose weight... Are you going to
ballet every day? I'm going to Club Med on the
11th for 4 days, I can't wait maybe I'll have a
4 day fling! Don't worry I won't get pregnant.
You'll be happy to hear that I've started knitting!
Now I won't bug you to knit me a sweater but
you still can if you want... PS I can't wait for a
big cuddle!

I just talked to you on the phone and I love you.
The first thing I want when I get through those
airport doors is a big, REAL cuddle. I started
crying tonight just for no reason and Dad com-
forted me which somehow made me feel worse....
I can't wait to see you again and I never thought
I'd say it but I miss your yelling. I went on a blind
date the other night! What an experience, actually mine was quite good looking (Keith) but the
other (I went with a friend) was a big sicko! They
were both English. Keith asked me out again but
I said 'no', I was scared that a 22 year old could
try to get me into bed. A horny man is hard to
stop you've always said. This weekend we're
going to Club Med so I still have a chance of
having a wild fling!

I love you so much and I'm glad that you're
you. You're one of a kind. I'll be expecting that
cuddle. Lots of love FOREVER, Sophie

SRI SATHYA SAI BABA

Sri Sathya Sai Baba was born Sathya Narayana Raju on November 23rd, 1926 in Puttaparthi, a remote village in South India. He is a divine Avatar. He was a brilliant child, but what made him unique was his extraordinary wisdom and compassion. When he was fourteen he declared that he would be known as Sai Baba and that his mission was to bring about the spiritual regeneration of humanity.

He established a model education system, which includes primary and secondary schools and an accredited university, offering undergraduate, graduate and doctoral degrees with no fees to the students. He has built four hospitals equipped with state-of-the-art technologies in cardiology and cardiothoracic surgery, neurology and neurosurgery, nephrology and urosurgery and ophthalmology. Thousands of surgeries have been performed absolutely free. He has developed massive drinking water projects bringing much-needed relief to millions of villagers.

Teacher and healer, diplomat and visionary, friend and comforter, Sai Baba is one of the most extraordinary spiritual leaders of our time. His motto is "Love All, Serve All."

In Toronto, I went to a meditation held weekly by three young men. One evening in 1986 they showed a video of Sai Baba, saying, "Once you hear about him he will come into your life." And he did. I have felt his presence and guidance ever since. No matter what I write, I can never do justice to Sai Baba.

Having heard so many stories about him and his miracles, I wanted to see Sai Baba for myself. In January 1998, I went with a British group to visit Sai Baba's ashram in Puttaparthi. I met all nine members of the group for the first time in Heathrow airport and on the plane. We all bonded,even though Ivan, the leader, was a terrible task master and organized us out of our minds.

We took off in a gigantic Air India plane. Smoking was allowed in the back! The food was delicious, chicken makhan-

SRI SATHYA SAI BABA

wala, and a dessert made with vermicelli, condensed milk and cardamon, called semiya malai. We changed planes in Mumbai and flew on to Bangalore where we stayed for two nights. I will include some of my diary.

Clare and Sylvia and I went out for four hours, with Farouk a taxi driver; rather he has a scooter on three wheels covered with a seat for us in the back. They look like dolls' prams. Hilarious and dangerous afternoon, shooting through incredible traffic on a collision course with cars, buses, trucks, bikes, people, children, everyone honking madly. Went to shops and got our WHITE outfits that Ivan insists we wear. We went for "taj mahal" tea at the wonderful Hotel Oberon and saw a HUGE acacia tree they call CACTUS. Clare is an interpreter in French and Arabic for Scotland Yard, and Sylvia is a painter from Venice living in Oxford.

The next day we drove to Puttaparthi and stayed in an hotel as the ashram was full. Clare and I had a room together with three beds, so we had lots of room. We were very disorganized. I was the only one in the group who had brought a sewing kit and was busy mending for everyone.

We had the funniest drama. At 4.15 a.m. I had just put on my underwear and Clare was in the bathroom, fully dressed. There was a shriek. Instead of flushing, she had turned a fitting and it had come right out of the wall. Water poured into the bathroom. I rushed in and sent her for help. I tried to stop it by putting my fingers into the broken pipe, which gave me a freezing cold shower so powerful I could hardly breathe. Terry came flying up and took off his nightshirt, so he only had his underwear on. I said, "I am half naked but come here quickly!" He told me to keep my fingers in the pipe and went to get more help. It was SO icy! I could hear Baba's voice saying,

160

"Well you wanted to have a shower." I had been too scared up till then, as the plumbing looked so dubious. The unfortunate night watchman came and took over until they turned the water off at the main. We went to Darshan suitably 'cleansed,' as Alex said.

I had woken up intent on taking Clare and moving to the Sai Towers Hotel, leaving the group at the other hotel. But after the shower, I knew I couldn't leave them. I laughed all day, and Terry and I have kept in touch. We will never forget that day.

We had another drama later, when Alex went wild, took his clothes off in the ashram garden and assaulted a policeman. He was promptly deported from India. George, his father-in-law, had to go with him. We were lucky we were not all deported.

We moved into the ashram. Ivan and Terry shared a room, and I was with Josette and Jay. Clare, Carole and Sylvia were together.

Here is my typical day: alarm set for 3.30 am but I wake at 2.15 having gone to sleep about 10:00 p.m.. We get dressed, leave 4.30 am and sit in the street on our cushions. It is still PITCH dark. 5.15 we go up to the temple and sit outside. 5.30 men are chanting the 21 Oms. Then they go round the temple chanting bhajans and tinkling cymbals, and we sit there till 6:00 a.m. Our shoes are all in a heap under a tree, and we run into the temple to wait for Baba. The birds are going berserk, and it's so peaceful. At 7.30 we go and have porridge, fruit salad, a piece of toast and peanut butter and tea. I skip the bhajans at 9:00 and get back into my old western clothes. It is a good time to catch up with laundry or shopping, till lunch at 12:00. Anything we do involves a long, long walk. Darshan is at 1.30 again in the heat of the day. The flagstones burn our feet as we dash into the temple. We have tea after darshan

SRI SATHYA SAI BABA

and usually go back to bhajans after that, before
having a shower. Then there is dinner, the meeting with the group, and bed. Tea is fun as we go
to Princes café—lovely things to eat there and
such good tea.

Carole and I copied this 'Thought for the Day.'

> Until the reality of the PARAMATMA is
> known you are over-powered and stunned by the
> uproar of the world. But once you enter deep
> into the realm of spiritual endeavour everything
> becomes clear and the knowledge of the reality
> awakens within you. Baba

The highlight for me was when Jo and I went up to see Sai
Gita, Baba's pet elephant. She was in the Boys' College waiting
for Baba to come out.

> She kept trumpeting and ringing her bell and
> it was getting dark before he came at last—she
> was ecstatic but we couldn't see him behind her.
> Suddenly a bus stopped at the gate and the col-
> lege students panicked in case there was a gun. I
> had anticipated pandemonium in the crowd, so I
> grabbed Jo and pulled her away just as the gates
> shot open and the boys came flying out yelling
> at the bus. They made a human chain for Baba's
> car to come out. We were all knocked back into
> each other. I hung on to Jo and our rickshaw boy
> grabbed my other hand and led us back to the
> rickshaw. We were right in the middle of every-
> thing, it was SO exciting. Everyone was hooting
> and honking, I just loved it. It was like being in
> a David Lean movie.

> I do feel at home here. But think I am re-living
> history at some level, knowing that whatever I
> want to happen will happen. India is so majestic
> and so squalid all at the same time. Loved step-
> ping into that TEEMING street in Puttaparthi,

162

losing myself in the din and clatter of traffic, vendors, beggars, bullock carts.

As I dozed in the plane to London felt Sai Baba encouraging me never to become attached to the form (his physical form). "If I'd smiled at you you'd have become attached to the form. LOOK for me in your HEART. LOOK for me in the eyes and hearts of people around you. I AM OMNIPRESENT OMNISCIENT, I AM ALL, I AM LOVE."

THE CUTTING FAMILY

Granny Plumb came from a very happy family. Her parents' marriage was made in heaven. The Reverend W. Aubrey Cutting, Vicar of Gayton in Norfolk, met Theresa Anne Cousins when they were children under a dining room table; they died within a week of each other in April 1893. They had two sons and seven daughters. My great grandfather was a cheerful soul who loved music and books more than anything. He had a distinguished academic career (Ipswich School and Corpus Christi College, Cambridge), and was a great rider and walker. He wrote a book for the parish called *Gleanings about Gayton in the Olden Time 1889*. His father and father before him were both doctors at Holbrook in Suffolk at the beginning of the nineteenth century.

The family sounds like Jane Austen with seven little girls skipping about after their father. They were Emma (my grandmother), Evelyn, Theresa, Fanny, Annie, Marcia and Beatrice. Emma married Charles Plumb. Evelyn married Dr. Norman Evans and had two daughters, Mamie and Bobby, who raised their families in South Africa. Mamie married Gordon Wills. We heard about them but only met Peter Wills, their handsome son, when he came to London. (Evelyn is buried in the ancient section of Hampstead Churchyard.) Marcia married a German gentleman in Pueblo, Colorado. Annie married Dr. F.H. Cotton Marshall of Leeds, and had three daughters, Ruth, Mary and Joan. I am including the detailed newspaper description of Annie's wedding. Fanny married Dr. Chadwick, an art connoisseur. They had no children. Another one became a nun. Annie died in 1914 when her daughters were still quite young.

The sons were Aubrey and Ernest. Ernest stayed in Norfolk and became a doctor. Aubrey went to the United States, settled in Colorado and raised cattle. His son George Cutting was friends with my father and often came to London. He settled in Warrenton, Virginia and became 'very wealthy even by American standards' according to my father. He married twice and had seven children altogether. I went to Warrenton for Thanksgiv-

164

THE CUTTING FAMILY

ing dinner in 1956 and met several of them.

My favourite of all my father's Cutting cousins was Aunt Annie's daughter Mary. In 1922 when she was twenty two she went to Canada telling everybody she was going round the world and would not be staying. However, she met Cecil Clark in Victoria and married him. They had three daughters, Joan, Pixie and Julie. I am very fond of them. We have kept in touch through the years. Mary settled in Victoria and lived a long and happy life. She was very welcoming and supportive to me when I first arrived in British Columbia in 1966. Her daughter Joan married Bud Smith and they had Julian and Sally. Now Sally has three children, Natasha, Alexandra, and Hamish. Pixie married Keith and had four children, Malcolm, Wendy, Ian, and Robin. Julie married and had Megan who has Julia. Julie is now married to Jim Sabiston. I have written down all the names I know of.

I heard that Mary's sister Ruth went to Africa and spent her life there. She was quite a pioneer says Julie, who met her and heard her stories about game hunting. Joan Marshall married Professor La Touche, a cancer specialist, of San Raphael, France. They had a son, Michael.

Here is the account of Annie Cutting's wedding:

> The marriage of Miss Annie Louise Cutting the fifth daughter of the late Reverend W.A. Cutting, Vicar of Gayton in this County, sister of Mr. E. Buxton Cutting, M.R.C.S., Chetwynd House, Stalham, with Mr. F.H. Cotton Marshall, B.A., of the Grammar School, Daventry, took place at the Parish Church, Stalham, on Thursday afternoon.
>
> The bride who entered the church leaning on the arm of her brother, was attired in a dress of ivory satin, trimmed with chiffon, with tulle veil and orange blossoms, carrying an exquisite shower bouquet composed of white blooms and maidenhair fern. The bridesmaids, the two youngest sisters of the bride, the Misses Beatrice

THE CUTTING FAMILY

and Marcia Cutting, wore dresses of white fig-
ured alpacca, trimmed with white satin and silver
braid, charming white felt picture hats, with
white and pink roses and ostrich tips, carrying
shower bouquets of pink carnations and roses.
Each wore a gold bracelet, the gift of the bridegroom. The bride was given away by her brother,
Dr. E. Buxton Cutting. Mr. Charles E. Hughes,
of St. Paul's Cathedral Choir School, London,
was best man. As the congregation assembled,
Mr. V. Spanton played W.H. Jude's "Processional
March." As the bridal party entered the church,
hymn 351, "How Welcome was the Call" was
sung. For the first time here the wedding party
took their places at the entrance to the chan-
cel. During the chanting of psalm CXXVIII,
the bride and bridegroom advanced to the Holy
Table. At the conclusion of the service, which
was impressively read by the Vicar, the Reverend
J. Neville White, the Reverend A.A.T. Crosse,
Vicar of Hickling gave an address. Previous to
the address, 'O Perfect Love, all human thought
transcending', was sung. The Reverend J. Neville White pronounced the Benediction. The only
decorations in the church were the altar vases,
which were filled with white blooms. After sign-
ing the Register, and as the bridal party left the
church, Miss Kathleen Rust played the 'Wedding
March' from 'Lohengrin.' The church was completely filled.

Immediately after the wedding ceremony, Dr.
and Mrs. Cutting held an 'At Home' at Chetwynd
House. The following invitations were issued:
The Reverend J. Neville and Mrs. White, Rev-
erend J. and Mrs. Fowler, Reverend A. and Mrs.
Groom, Reverend A.J. and Mrs. Alvis, Reverend
H. and Mrs. Ffolkes, Reverend A.A.T. and Mrs.
Crosse, Reverend J.F. and Mrs. Kendall, Rever-

166

THE CUTTING FAMILY

end G. and Mrs. Holloway, the Misses Holloway and Mrs. Whitehead. Reverend R.A. and Mrs. Hitchkock, Mr. F. Clowes, J.P., and party, Mr and Mrs. E. Slipper, Miss Paterson, Mr. and Mrs. R.E. Smith, Mr. and Miss Harding, Mrs. Gladden and party, Mrs. F. Powell, and Mr. and Mrs. Dann and party. The wedding cake was supplied by Buzsard, Oxford Street, London.

At 4oc Mr. and Mrs. Marshall left for Hunstanton. The bride's costume de voyage consisted of green cloth with pink vest and a very pretty toque of pink and black. There was a large concourse to witness their departure, and as the train left the station a plentiful supply of fog signals announced to those afar off that the bride and bridegroom had started on their honeymoon with the best wishes of all for their future happiness.

The bride's presents consisted of gold curb bracelet from the bridegroom. Clock, Miss Cutting. Cheque, Miss Theresa Cutting. Breakfast service, Miss Emma Cutting. Cutlery and cheque, Miss Beatrice Cutting. Silver salt cellars, Miss Marcia Cutting. Afternoon kettle stand, Dr. E.B. and Mrs. Cutting. Household plate, Dr. and Mrs. Evans. Household linen, Mrs. Marshall. Dessert knives and forks, Reverend and Mrs. Boyd. Carvers, Miss Helen and Master Jack Boyd. Dinner service, Mr. and Mrs. James Weston. Cheque, Miss Cobon. Silver pot, Mrs. C. Buxton. Dessert spoons, Miss Fison. Silver napkin rings, Reverend E, and Mrs. Symonds. Two pairs of green glass vases, Miss Emmeline Ambrose. Scalloped Worcester dishes, Mrs. Hicks. Calendar, Mrs. Broad. Travelling cup, Miss Broad. Silver sugar basin and cream jug, Lady Charlotte Arnold. Emerald ring, Mrs. J. Weston. Silver tea kettle,

167

THE CUTTING FAMILY

Mr. and Miss Harding. Silver toast rack and butter dish combined, Mr. and Mrs. George Rix. Toast rack, Mrs. P. Powell. Fruit spoons, Mrs. Gladden. Silver sugar tongs, Reverend A.A.T. and Mrs. Crosse. Album, Miss Booth. Engraving, Reverend A. and Mrs. Groom. Buttonhook, Mrs. Crawford. Bread trencher, Betsey Smith.

Those of the bridegroom: Gold watch chain, the bride. Gold pencil case, Miss Cutting. Gold links and studs, Miss B. Cutting. Sugar basin, Mrs. Ffolkes. Silver spoon, Mr. B. Hamblin Smith. Claret jug and cups, Mr. and Mrs. Bouchier. Cheque, Mr. and Mrs. Ambrose. Revolving book case, Mr. Bensley. Apocrypha, Mrs. Bensley. Mr. and Mrs. White, purse and guinea.

So how do I know our great grandparents' marriage was so happy? I have noticed that the Cuttings have something very special, a wonderful optimistic outlook on life that I wish I had. Granny Plumb, my father and Mary Clark all had this lovely quality, and so have her daughters.

THE GAGE FAMILY

The Family Tree of the Irish Gages starts with Sir John Gage who married Elinor, daughter and co-heiress of Thomas Synt. Clere, of Heighton St. Clere in Sussex and Aston Clinton in Bucks. Sir John acquired several manors including Penshurst and Burstowe. He was knighted by Edward IV and died September 30, 1475.

Their elder son, William, married Agnes Bolney and this marriage began the English Gages of Firle and Hengrave.

Their younger son, John, married Margaret Tawyer. Five generations later John Gage and his wife Elizabeth Smyth moved their family to Magilligan, Co. Londonderry in 1661. Four generations later, my great great grandfather, William Charles Gage was born in 1810. He married Mary Olphert. They lived in Drummond, Ballykelly, Co. Londonderry, and had four children. Their eldest son Conolly Marcus, was born in 1839 and he married Mary Victoria Reeves. (I still have two diamond rings that belonged to her.)

My grandfather, William Charles, was born in 1877. He had two younger sisters Armande and Juliet. I met Auntie Armande; she was sweet and funny. At that time I was engaged to a third cousin, Marcus Baillie Gage who lived in Dublin. She looked up at me grinning wickedly, and said "will he DO Valerie?." Actually he did not. She married the Reverend Wilfred Dixon and had one son, Conolly. He was a dear kind man and a good friend to all of us. He lived until he was almost 92. The family lived in Coleraine Co. Londonderry.

My grandfather married May Gurney Holmes in 1904. Conolly Hugh was born in 1905 and Mary Violet (my mother) was born January 21, 1907.

Juliet and I went to Drummond House in Ballykelly (now a huge hotel), where our great great grandparents lived. We visited the parish church, Tamlaghtfinlagan Church, where there

169

THE GAGE FAMILY

are several plaques in their memory. The family vault is in the churchyard. The family motto is *Courage Sans Peur.*

Uncle Conolly married Elinor Nancy Martyn in 1932. They had two children, Gillian Nancy in 1935, and William Marcus in 1938. We used to play with them when we were staying with Granny. They were the only children we knew and we keep in touch. Conolly was a barrister and a Member of Parliament for Belfast. Granny used to call him every night after dinner to tell him the questions she wanted him to ask in the House of Commons. After that he became a judge.

Gillian (Jink) married Richard Morris-Adams in 1958 and had James Egerton (Tod) in 1959, Deborah Margaret (Debbie) in 1961 and Conolly Richard (Olly) in 1968. William (Bill) married Penelope Groves in 1962. They had Conolly Marcus in 1964, Timothy Charles in 1966 and Hugh William James in 1970. Bill was a barrister, then a judge in the High Court, and now he is Lord Justice of Appeal in the Supreme Court.

Tim Gage married Diana Campbell. They live in Vancouver so we often get together. Bill and Penny Gage and Hugh Gage and Holly Rowland come to visit and I love seeing them. Marcus married Pauline and has William and Jessica. Tod Morris-Adams married Cathy Anderson. They went round the world and came to stay with me in Toronto. They live in Somerset and have four sons, Hugo, Charlie, Joe and Edward. Debbie Morris-Adams married Sam Laidlaw and has three sons, Arthur, Humphrey and Fergus, and a daughter Clementine. Olly Gage married Amy Streeter and they have Sam.

Mary, my mother had three daughters, Valerie, Juliet, and Perdita. Juliet married Richard Moyle and had Justin, Hamish, and Toby. Justin married Alex and had Emily. Hamish is an artist who lives in Ireland. Toby married Heather and had Marley. Perdita married Vernon Robinson and had Armande. Valerie married Bill Mair and had Ben, Lucy, and Sophie. Ben married Laura Leslie and had Gage and Emma. Lucy married Stewart Houchen. Sophie married Trevor Sosin and had Gracie and Andrew.

THE GAGE FAMILY

Granny Gage would be so proud if she could see all the lovely children their marriage produced. They had five grandchildren, thirteen great grandchildren, and seventeen great great grandchildren.

THE GAGE FAMILY

THE LANDED GENTRY OF IRELAND

GAGE *formerly* OF WILLBROOK HOUSE

CONOLLY HUGH GAGE, of Fruit Hill, Widdington, Saffron Walden, Essex, Dep.-Chm. Essex Quarter Sessions, M.P. for S. Belfast, 1945-51, Chancellor of the Dioceses of Coventry and Lichfield, Barrister-at-law, Inner Temple 1930, Recorder of Saffron Walden and Malden 1948-49, served in World War II (despatches), A.D.J.A.G., Lt.-Col. 1st Canadian Army, formerly Gnr. (T.A.); *b.* 10 Nov. 1905, *educ.* Repton, and Sidney Sussex Coll. Camb. (B.A. 1928, M.A. 1948), *m.* 6 Sept. 1932, ●Elinor Nancy, dau. of William Edward Martyn, of Wimbledon, Surrey, and has issue,

●WILLIAM MARCUS, *b.* 22 April, 1938, *educ.* Repton.
●Gillian Nancy, *b.* 29 Sept. 1935.

LINEAGE—WILLIAM GAGE, of Bellarena, Co. Londonderry, *m.* Anne, dau. of Thomas Church, of Kilrea, Co. Londonderry, and had issue,

THOMAS GAGE, of Bellarena, *m.* 1713, Sarah, dau. of John Hodson, of Bovagh, and had issue,
1. John, *d.s.p.*
2. Hodson, *m.* Sydney, dau. of Acheson Moore, and *d.* 1777, leaving issue, one dau., who *d. unm.*
3. William, *d.s.p.*
1. ELIZABETH, of whom presently.

His dau.,
ELIZABETH GAGE, of Bellarena, *m.* 10 Feb. 1742, CONOLLY McCAUSLAND, of Fruit Hill, Co. Londonderry, and had issue,
MARCUS GAGE, of Bellarena, adopted the name of GAGE in accordance with his mother's will, *b.* 1755, *m.* 24 Jan. 1788, Julia Stirling (*d.* 1839), and *d.* 1815, leaving issue,
1. Conolly, of Bellarena.
2. WILLIAM CHARLES, of whom presently.

The yr. son,
WILLIAM CHARLES GAGE, of Drummond House, Ballykelly, Co. Londonderry, *b.* 1810, *m.* 1838, Mary, dau. of Rev. John Olphert, of Falcarragh, Co. Donegal, and *d.* 1882, leaving issue,
1. CONOLLY MARCUS, of whom presently.
2. Olphert, *m.* Elizabeth Barnham, and had issue.
Hildebrand.
1. Julia, *m.* 11 Aug. 1864, George Miller Harvey, D.L., J.P., son of John Harvey, of Malin Hall, Malin, Co. Donegal (*see that family*), and *d.* 8 April, 1912, leaving issue, one son and two daus. He *d.* 13 June, 1919.
2. Lizzie, *m.* H. R. Scott, son of John Scott, of Somerset, Coleraine, Co. Londonderry, and *d.* 1892.

The elder son,
CONOLLY MARCUS GAGE, of Drummond House, Ballykelly, Co. Londonderry, J.P., *b.* 1839, *m.* 1866, Victoria (*d.* 17 March, 1917), dau. of William Studdert Reeves, of Rosedale, Shankhill, Co. Dublin, and *d.* 1924, leaving issue,
1. WILLIAM CHARLES, of whom presently.
1. Juliet, *m.* Stewart Olphert, son of John Olphert, of Eglinton, Co. Londonderry, and *d.s.p.* 12 Nov. 1932.
2. Armande, *m.* 21 Nov. 1911, ●Rev. Wilfred Craig Dixon, M.A., formerly Rector of Balteagh, Co. Londonderry (*Franfort, Lodge Road, Coleraine, Co. Londonderry*), son of late Wakefield Haughton Dixon, of Dunowen, Cliftonville, Belfast, and *d.* 30 Dec. 1955, leaving issue, one son,

The only son,
WILLIAM CHARLES GAGE, of Willbrook House, Rathfarnham, Co. Dublin, and of Felden, Whitehouse, Co. Antrim, *b.* 1878, *educ.* Coleraine, and Trin. Coll. Dublin, *m.* 28 Dec. 1904, May Gurney (*d.* 6 June, 1953), dau. of Rt. Hon. Lord Justice Hugh Holmes, of 3, Fitzwilliam Place, Dublin, and *d.* 3 May, 1947, leaving issue,
CONOLLY HUGH, of whom we treat.
●Mary Violet, *b.* 21 Jan, 1907, *m.* 1stly, 17 Feb. 1931 (*m. diss* by div. 1939), Charles Theodore Plumb, only son of late Rt. Rev. Charles Edward Plumb, D.D., Bishop of St. Andrews, Dunkeld, and Dunblane, and has issue, two daus. She *m.* 2ndly, 8 Oct. 1939, Capt. John Richard Anthony Nicholson, 1st Bn. Leicestershire Regt., only son of John Percy Nicholson, of Leicester, and has further issue, one dau. He was *k.* in action, 16 July, 1944. She *m.* 3rdly, 25 Sept. 1954, ●Hugh Andrew Holmes (3, *Melina Place, St. John's Wood, N.W.8*), only son of late Sir Valentine Holmes, Q.C.
RESIDENCE—Fruit Hill, Widdington, Saffron Walden, Essex. *Clubs*—Carlton; Ulster (Belfast).

172

THE HOLMES FAMILY

Hugh Holmes, my great grandfather, lived from 1840 until 1919. There is no record of his parents, and he was brought up by two aunts. My great grandmother, Olivia Moule, was born March 27, 1843 and lived until January 21, 1901. They married in 1869 and had seven children: William (b. 1871), May (Granny) (b. June 27, 1873), Elsie (b. 1876), Violet (b. 1878), Alice (b. 1880), Hugh (b. 1883) and Valentine (b. 1886).

I heard lots of stories about them, but knew just one: William's only daughter, Olivia, who was my mother's great friend. She married Peter Hogg and had Jocelyn, Jeremy, and Adam. I saw Granny's three sisters only when they were old. Granny never seemed to be old, yet she was the eldest. Her mother died in 1901, and she took on responsibility for the family.

I never met Uncle Hugh, who married Rose Falls, but met two of their daughters, Hilary and Imogen, and liked them very much. Hilary later married her first cousin, James Henry, who was Aunt Violet's eldest son. Cousins often married in this family. We got to know Uncle Val's family. He married Gwendoline Armstrong, and they had two children, Hugh and Jane. They were very, very quiet and reserved. Uncle Val and Uncle Hugh were knighted at the same time and met at Buckingham Palace. They were astonished, neither one having told the other. Uncle Val loved going to the dog races and was rarely at home. When I did meet him we talked about murder mysteries. Nearly all the Holmes men were lawyers. Hilary said to me at my mother's funeral, "Those Holmes women are made of steel."

Most of the previous generation has passed away. By writing this, I hope to make it easier to follow the threads. More about the Holmes family can be found in the section about the Moule family, and those references may make it easier to trace ancestors.

One Man in His Time written by Hugh Holmes, tells much more about my great grandfather's career. Here are excerpts:

173

THE HOLMES FAMILY

My father and mother's ancestors had both come to Ireland in the Seventeenth Century. Gabriel of The Holme came from Cumberland and had served in Cromwell's Ironsides, for which he was rewarded by a grant of land in Donegal... My grandfather—Lord Justice Hugh Holmes, had been born in Dongannon, Co. Tyronne, and had gone to Trinity College, Dublin. He was called to the Bar and thereafter carved out a most successful career as Lord Justice of Appeal, later joining Lord Salisbury's government via University seat at Westminster. There he became Attorney General for Ireland and was continually involved in Home Rule Legislation.

During most of his career he lived in Fitzwilliam Square in Dublin, and though he was comfortably off, like many successful lawyers, he was incompetent in matters of finance and consequently left very little money when he died. He had lost most of it by investing his assets in the Royal Mail Steam Packet Company, a worldfamous shipping line which crashed as a result of a great embezzlement scandal involving its chairman, Lord Kylsant.

My grandfather wrote some personal memoirs covering a very interesting period of his distinguished life, especially in relation to the part he played as Attorney General of Ireland, at Westminster, when events led up to the creation of the Irish Free State.

As one who believes strongly in the significance of the meaning and influence of the family in the affairs of the human race, it seems to me that the recorded knowledge of progressive generations of any family must create a significant continuity factor which can only strengthen the confidence and stability of its individuals. The more

174

THE HOLMES FAMILY

an individual can relate to other people, the more meaningful life must be.

I found a couple of pages from a book *The Old Munster Circuit* by Maurice Healy. He says:

> Hugh Holmes was short, bearded and looked like a severe edition of Father Christmas attempting to disguise himself as a retired admiral! He was a silent man, of very deep feelings, which he rarely showed... He took a very severe view of agrarian crime; and he showed no pity to the perpetrators when they were convicted before him. One elderly prisoner staggered when he heard himself sentenced to fifteen years' penal servitude. "Ah! My Lord," he cried, "I'm a very old man, and I'll never do that sentence!" Most people in court were moved; not so the judge. "Well," said he, "try to do as much of it as you can!
>
> The Holmeses and the Murphys (Mr. Justice Murphy's family) were inter-married almost as much as the Healys and the Sullivans; He has given a younger son, Valentine, to the English Bar, and also a grandson, Sir James Henry, whose father Denis, was Attorney-General for Ireland, and afterwards the first Lord Chief Justice of Northern Ireland.

Denis Henry married Granny's sister, Violet. I met their son James when he was married to Hilary Holmes, Hugh Holmes' daughter. She was sister to the Hugh who wrote *One Man in his Time*. They had three daughters. Harold Murphy married Granny's sister, Elsie, and Edward Murphy married Granny's other sister, Alice. Later, in 1953, my mother married her first cousin Hugh Holmes, Uncle Val's son.

My great grandfather must have been intimidating to meet and try to talk to. But his personal memoir is very hard to put down and shows what a deep thinking and feeling man he was.

175

THE HOLMES FAMILY

He wrote:

> It was in the afternoon of the 30th May 1868
> and in the drawing-room of John Monroe's
> house in Mountjoy Square that I first met Olivia
> Moule.

He writes at length about all the circumstances that led up
to this meeting in Olivia's sister's (Lizzie's) house. Several pages
later:

> My recollection is that Olivia was alone in the
> drawing-room, playing the piano and having
> her hat on, when I was shown into the room.
> Although nothing could have been further from
> my thoughts than love or matrimony, I looked
> at her with some interest, for I fully understood
> that the honey-moon was still shining on John
> and Lizzie and that for the next three days Miss
> Moule and myself would be largely dependent
> on each other for enjoyment. My first impres-
> sions were distinctly pleasant. She had no claim
> to beauty, indeed if she had I should not have
> been so well satisfied, for, according to my
> experience, handsome women often forget that
> 'beauty lives with kindness.' Her old carte-de-
> visite photograph in a striped dress and walking
> costume gives the best idea of her as she was
> then. She looked much younger than her sister,
> and in many points of appearance they were a
> contrast to each other.
>
> She was a decided 'blonde' with pink and white
> cheeks and very light brown hair falling in ring-
> lets around her head. She had a cheerful happy
> looking face, and there was a cordial ring in her
> voice. Her accent was free from even the slightest
> touch of Cockneyism and she spoke fluently and
> without affectation, but with a quaint mannerism
> of utterance which in those days others as well
> as myself thought piquant and attractive. This

THE HOLMES FAMILY

afterwards gradually disappeared with her continued residence in Ireland.

She liked to see men—especially young men—well groomed and tidy and had a strong objection to any want of manner on their part. She also criticized severely any neglect of those deferences and attentions which are due from men to women. I fear that in both these respects I fell far short of her standard. Amongst other defects of costume I wore a ragged watch-chain of leather which she afterwards told me she found it hard to get over, but which nevertheless she preserved all her life as a souvenir of that happy time.

Brought up as I was without Mother or companion of my own age, in an atmosphere of sombre, although not unkindly Puritanism; left by my Father's death my own master before I was twenty with but slender means to prepare myself for my profession, living for the greater part of every year alone or with male companions, it might be thought that I should have few ideas in common with a girl whose youth had been brightened by the sunshine of strong family affection, whose home was well endowed with this world's goods, and who had never known care or responsibility. Yet from the first everything went smoothly with us.

She was always looked upon as the sentimental one of the family. She lived more in day-dreams and had more enthusiasm than the rest. She often said that she could not remember a time when her youth was not brightened by an element of romance. ...She had many little love passages, too earnest to be called flirtations, but too short-lived to be serious...Without doubt the most attractive feature of her nature was her warmth of heart and capacity for love and

177

THE HOLMES FAMILY

friendship... It may seem strange to those who generally saw her bright and joyous, to hear that the predominant note in her nature was a serious one. Her whole life was pervaded with feeling her responsibility to a Higher Power. She was a simple-minded believing Christian.

She was devoted to her eldest son Willie, and visited him when he was away at school as often as she could. He is mentioned more than any of the other children.

This unpublished book is amazing. The 232 pages cover everything under the sun in great detail. Uncle Conolly (mother's brother) wrote and told me that:

> Three chapters of Grandfather's book (the political ones) were published in Irish Historical Studies by two very bright young historians, Dr. Vincent and Alastair Cooke. They published it just as it was written, with of course copious notes and explanatory matter. They said it was remarkably accurate and have used it in other books they have written. Incidentally they discovered that Winston Churchill had access to it when he wrote the life of Lord Randolph. The rest of the book may well be of interest to future historians writing on social matters of that period.

THE MOULE FAMILY

Francis Moule and Anne Watkins were my great great great grandparents. I was four when I saw their portraits and became obsessed with them. Now I feel even more connected to them. They lived in Sneads Green House in a village called Elmley Lovett in Worcestershire.

The book *Elmley Lovett and the Moules of Sneads Green* written by a cousin, Horace Monroe, starts with Edward the Confessor and moves through Plantaganet, Tudor and Stuart times to the present day. The property was owned by the Earls of Warwick and then Henry VIII who sold it to Sir Robert Acton. He had four daughters who divided it up when they married. However what with one marriage and another, eventually John Moule (b. 1673) owned the whole estate, and was able to pass it on through the generations. His great grandfather Francis Moule, who married Margaret Boyse in 1575, was the first Moule to be recorded on the family tree.

The book is a fascinating account of history and human beings. How they lived and loved and hated and fought and died, as people do. There were village disputes over land and money just as there are now. Then there was a Civil War, and battles took place in Worcestershire. John Moule's great grandson Francis (b. 1768) married Anne Watkins in April 1791, the year Mozart died, during the days of the French Revolution.

They had nine children. Their son Francis inherited Sneads Green. John Watkins Moule, their second son, lived from 1796 to 1879, married Jane Harvie in 1828, and had nine children. Francis had no children so he left the property to his three unmarried sisters, Anne, Elizabeth and Olive. They left it to two of John Watkins Moule's daughters. His youngest daughter, Caroline, inherited Sneads Green House and it passed to her daughter, Laura Ellen Stocks, whose descendants probably still live there. His eighth child, Olivia (b. 1843) was my great grandmother. I heard a lot about her and her sister Elizabeth, known as Lizzie.

179

THE MOULE FAMILY

They went everywhere together and married Irish barristers, John Monroe and Hugh Holmes (my great grandfather). The gentlemen both became judges of the High Court of Justice in Ireland and members of Her Majesty's Privy Council. They each had seven children. Elizabeth's third son, Horace (who wrote the book) was Dean's Vicar of St. Patrick's Cathedral, Dublin, and Canon of Southwark. Her daughter Edith married Walter Broadben. They had four children: Ione, John, Moira and Hubert.

Olivia and Hugh Holmes' children were William, May, Elsie, Violet, Alice, Hugh and Valentine. William married Dorothy Fowle and had a daughter Olivia; May married William Gage and had Conolly and Mary (my mother); Elsie married Harold Murphy and had Richard, Daphne and June; Violet married Denis Henry and had James, Olive, Alice, Denis and Lorna; Alice married Edward Murphy; I remember her being very old and ill when I was little; Hugh married Rose Falls; they had Hilary, Hugh, Rosamund, Imogen and Valentine; Hilary's husband was killed in the war, but she had a second happy marriage with James Henry, her first cousin. We used to visit them. Valentine (the youngest of Olivia's children) married Gwendoline Armstrong and they had Hugh and Jane. We saw a lot of Auntie Gwen, she was a lovely sweet lady. Hugh later married his first cousin, my mother. Jane married Sylvan Van de Weyer; they had three sons: Mark, Andrew and Robert. I keep in touch with Mark who lives in London.

We never saw much of my mother's generation but heard lots of stories about them and met several at her funeral. I have written more about the people I know, but have put in these details for the benefit of future generations who may wish to track their ancestors. It must be very confusing to read.

As this chapter is about marriages, I must mention Eric Whittome who married Ione Broadbent, Elizabeth Moule's granddaughter. He was a very special man with great integrity and very wise about life and marriage. We often went to stay with them on their fruit farm in Henfield, Sussex. They had three boys, Derek, Donald, and Peter who made me laugh. It is hard to believe only Donald is still alive.

THE MOULE FAMILY

When Ione died in 1966 Eric wrote a lovely book about her, called *Ione Whittome—A Memoir*. Later he married Betty who was wonderful for him. He gave me away at my wedding and was always there for me. Someone interviewed him about marriage. He said "When you get old two things face you. You either mellow or you get cantankerous and pernickety. You must have complete freedom and confidence in each other. Honesty is essential, frankness is vital. Marrying a second time is a compliment to the first wife, repeating a very happy experience."

After he died, his second wife, Betty, wrote:

> But what really sustained our incredible relationship (and I sometimes regretted having to sacrifice a more adventurous and successful academic career), was his marvellous openness and intellectual honesty with me. He could have changed the world, Valerie! He had such an honest, open mind and such wisdom! I didn't always agree with him but I could talk to him like talking to myself.

THE PLUMB FAMILY

The Plumbs originally came from Holland to settle in a village called Terrington St. Clements, near Kings Lynn in Norfolk. Most of them lived into their nineties.

Abraham Plumb was born in Kings Lynn on March 17, 1786. Jane Beckett (his wife) was born in Watlington on February 22, 1793.

Abraham and Jane were my great great grandparents and had nine children. Their seventh child, Abraham, was my great grandfather. I think he was a merchant and a great wheeler dealer. He was the one who sold timber to the Russians. He sounds like a powerful chauvinist who expected all his sons to be like him, so he must have been stunned when his son Charles decided to go into the Church.

Abraham was born July 13, 1830 and died April 7, 1910. He married Mary Claxton and they had ten children, six sons and four daughters.

Their daughters were Kathleen, Ada, Louise and Helen. Kathleen was not well. Helen never married. Louise married Basil Chambers, a minister in Bath who eventually became Basil Plumb's (her nephew's) godfather. Ada married Doctor Bryant and died in Bradford on Avon.

Their son Charles was my grandfather, born in 1865 and died in Edinburgh on November 26, 1930, a year and a half before I was born. I only met Uncle Harold who died in Bristol in 1962 aged 93. He was very interesting and had never married. Martin and Thomas went to Canada, to British Columbia and Alberta, but I think they lost touch with each other. This is why so many Plumbs scattered about Canada may not realize the others are there! Except for Ada Woods (née Plumb), but now I have lost track of her. John went to South Africa, and Clarkson lived in Ruislip; he married Hilda and had a son Robert who married Dorothea. Martin died in Vancouver before we got there, but we met

182

THE PLUMB FAMILY

his wife Aunt Lydia (Cozens) and two of their children, Basil and Ruth Plumb. Ruth says there is an eleventh child Alfred who had an accident with a train but I cannot find him in my records. Basil married Sheila; they had Jonas and Christine. Ruth married Colin Hempsall. They live in West Vancouver, but sadly Basil died in October 2005 just before his eightieth birthday.

Basil was a distinguished dentist. He was a fellow of both the International College of Dentistry, and the American College of Dentistry, as well as being a prosthodontist and member of many specialized dental associations to do with every aspect of dentistry.

Margaret Plumb, my father's sister, married Bernard Cook. They had David, Felicity and Angela. Felicity lives in England near her children, Philip and Gabby. Angela lives in Spain and has four daughters, Itziar, Esther, Mary Jo, Angela, and a son Ion.

Thomas Plumb, who went to Alberta, married Florence Jardine and had four children, Francis, Harold, Roger and Flora. Francis married Marion Collin and had Thomas, Ada and Irma. Harold married Muriel Collins and had Margaret and Sandra. Roger married Olive Mitchell and had Alan, Gordon and Dale. Flora married Don Morphy and had Don.

These marriages produced eighteen children, who are third cousins to my children. We met Ada, my second cousin, in Napanee. She married John Woods and has three sons, Thomas, Scott and Donald. She was wonderful and went to Terrington St. Clements in Norfolk where she did all sorts of research on the Plumb family.

BIBLIOGRAPHY

Cutting, Reverend W. Aubrey. *Gleanings about Gayton in the Olden Time 1889*. Norwich: Rampant Horse Street, 1889.

Eddy, Mary Baker. *Science and Health with Key to the Scriptures*

Fraser, Keath. *The Voice Gallery, Travels with a Glass Throat.*

Healy, Maurice. *The Old Munster Circuit.* London: Michael Joseph. 1948.

Hugh Holmes. *One Man in His Time.*

Marquis, Don. *archy's life of mehitabel.* New York: Doubleday, 1933.

Millman, Dan. *Sacred Journey of the Peaceful Warrior.* New World Library, 1991.

Monroe, Horace. *Elmley Lovett and the Moules of Sneads Green.*

Plumb, Charles. *The Satires of Juvenal* (verse translation). 1968.

------------------*Toward the Sun.* London: Parry Jackman, 1956.

------------------*These.* Charles Plumb. 1970

------------------*Walking in the Grampians.* London Alexander Maclehose & Co., 1935.

The Cat Sat on the Mat

Rehm, Diana. *Finding My Voice.* Alfred A. Knopf, Inc., 1999.

Yanagi, Soetsu. *The Unknown Craftsman.* Kodansha, Inc. 1972.

Printed in the United States
140628LV00004B/2/P